CONSCIOUS COURTSHIP

About the Author

Raymond Switzer is a Canadian psychologist, married with three children. He has extensive experience working with couples and with Canada's First Nations peoples. He now lives in Hungary where he has a private practice as a therapist. In the past twelve years he and his wife, Furugh Switzer, have given seminars and workshops throughout Europe. His avocation is music and he has recently recorded a CD of guitar music, primarily of his own compositions, entitled *Accents of My Soul*.

CONSCIOUS COURTSHIP

Finding Someone to Love for the Rest of Your Life

Raymond Switzer

GEORGE RONALD PUBLISHER
OXFORD

George Ronald, *Publisher*
Oxford
www.grbooks.com

ISBN: 978-0-85398-508-2

A catalogue record for this book is available from the British Library

Typeset by Magheross Graphics, France & Ireland *www.magheross.com*

Printed and bound in Great Britain by
Biddles Ltd, King's Lynn, Norfolk

Contents

Acknowledgements

My deepest and most heartfelt gratitude goes to my dear wife Furugh. So intertwined are we on the subjects of love and marriage that my thoughts and feelings on these subjects have become virtually inseparable from hers. In addition to her unfailing inspiration and encouragement, she has read the drafts of each chapter and offered many helpful insights and suggestions.

A special acknowledgement is also due to my friend and colleague, Dr. Ajang Farid. We came up with the idea of writing this book together and, initially, we started writing it together. Some of his contributions have, in one form or other, found their way into my final text. The basic outline of the book was also his idea and I have mostly adhered to it. I doubt the project would otherwise have got started at all, and in this, and for his continued support of the project after bowing out, I owe Ajang my greatest appreciation.

Of the many great psychologists and thinkers to have influenced me over the years, the most recent and significant to this present work is Harville Hendrix. Both through his books and through the training I have received in Imago Relationship Therapy I have gained a deeper understanding of the dynamics of love in marriage and of the psychological significance of the marital bond.

I would also like to thank those I have worked with as a therapist over the years. I have learned more from my clients than most would suspect and I believe this is the case with most therapists. The case studies in this book are based on real life, although names and situations have been changed.

Humour has its own special way of opening us up to the recognition of truths that might otherwise elude us, or to which we might otherwise stay closed. For this reason, I have liberally used humorous quotations throughout this book and have borrowed most heavily from one bilingual volume entitled *Ha elhagysz, veled mehetek?* (If you leave me, can I come too?), published by Cartaphilus Press in Hungary. This book, which contains quotations about the family, collected and translated by Gábor Salamon and Melinda Zalotay, deserves special mention here.

Finally, special thanks go to my editor, May Hofman, for her wise and helpful suggestions and her tireless efforts in trying to track down the most accurate references for quotations found on the Internet. May has edited some of the best books I have ever read and it was a special honour for me to have her working with me and editing this humble contribution of my own.

Introduction

Finding and having a partner is one of the most deeply engaging and fulfilling processes of our lives. It is also one of the most challenging. Life is full of paradoxes like this. We enter the mating arena full of excitement and anticipation; at the same time we experience doubt and shake with fear. When we are born – though we don't remember it – our first yearning is for connection, a reaching out for the breast of our mother. We need to be held. Our deepest anxieties – though we don't remember this either – are that our caregiver will not be there. When we begin the passage into adulthood, finding a partner recapitulates this primal scene from our babyhood. We yearn to have someone who will love us perfectly, yet we fear that this may not come to pass and we will be alone in the world.

These are unconscious mechanisms. As humans we **always** long for connection, but sometimes we develop a protective stance of denial concerning this basic need. Even those who are awake to the need to connect are not usually aware that we are all unconsciously looking for someone who will provide us with our unmet needs from childhood. This is not a sickness or a pathology; it is a natural yearning to achieve completeness.

This yearning for connection which shows itself in our desire to find a partner is much more than a physical or sexual urge, although these can be powerful in themselves. Our hope of finding a loving partner is a deep psychological longing which is full of meaning. The fulfilment of this hope has the potential to heal our feelings of loneliness and alienation. But it is even more than this – it is part of our spiritual quest, the conscious human journey towards unity, a unity which is the outward expression of our intrinsic oneness.

· · · · · · · · · ·

Our separateness is an illusion;
we are interconnected parts of the whole –
we are a pond with movement and memory.
Our reality is larger than you or me . . .

Ervin Laszlo

· · · · · · · · · ·

Everything is connected. We, and all that is in the universe, come from the same source. In the process of diversification and complexification which all creation is undergoing, the emergence of human consciousness is the crowning process. Only the unique capacity of human consciousness is capable of reflecting on our interconnectedness. All things are in relationship with all other things, but only humans **create** relationships. And only humans can feel alienated from creation. When a man and a woman find each other, form bonds of love and affection, and vow to stay together and to raise children together, they are setting the stage for a process which is intrinsic to the human spiritual journey. If we stay true to this process in the loving relationship, we will learn the most fundamental and profound lessons of unity.

· · · · · · · · · ·

Man who gets paid on Tuesday and is usually broke by Friday
would like to meet woman
who is paid on Friday and is usually broke by Tuesday.

Steve Allen

· · · · · · · · · ·

The attraction of opposites is intrinsic to nature's design. Falling in love is the peak of human feeling. Finding a partner is part of the grand design of the universe. Why then do we need a book? Let's face it – this is not the only book. There are thousands upon thousands of books on relationships. The fact is, we humans have grown confused and anxious over the issue. There are ever more potential partners – and myriad ways of finding them – yet people are finding it harder to really connect. Relationships, once made, are increasingly prone to fall apart. Couples who stay together seem more often than not to be unfulfilled in their relationship. Questions that single people have betray despair over their failure – or fear of failure – to find a fulfilling relationship.

Questions

The following are some of the questions generated in just a few minutes at the beginning of a seminar my wife Furugh and I recently gave:

1 I'm tired of going through romance again and again. What can I do to find a lasting fulfilling relationship?

2 How long should you take to get to know someone before you decide to marry?

3 How important are looks and physical attraction?

4 Everyone shows their best face during courtship. How can you really get to know another person?

5 I don't like talkative, dominant women. Is there a problem with this?

6 When do you know you love yourself enough that you are ready for marriage?

7 What happens if you have high expectations in looking for a partner? Is having high expectations of a partner's spirituality legitimate?

8 What do you do about fearing rejection?

9 How can I overcome my fear of not choosing wisely?

10 What are the essential qualities to look for in another? How do you recognize them?

11 The tide of society seems to be going against making clear choices or being careful. How can I be different?

12 What is the importance of finding someone who shares your religion?

13 How can I get my boyfriend interested in books on relationships?

14 What can you do about difficulties communicating with the other sex?

15 When is the right time to marry?

16 What about sharing responsibilities in a relationship?

17 How can you avoid playing games in relationships or in finding a partner?

18 What about having close relationships with someone who is not your partner?

19 What about differences in age, culture, or nationality?

20 What about dealing with your partner's personal or family problems?

21 How can you maintain your sense of self in a relationship and yet be engaged with the other?

22 When do you know you have found the right person?

These questions, we know, are just the tip of the iceberg. We are asked a wide array of questions relating to courtship whenever the subject is raised. I like this kind of questioning. It shows that people want to bring more consciousness to bear on some age-old problems. Many of the questions reveal the influence of social patterns. Some show the influence of certain kinds of trendy psychological thinking. Some of these questions would not have been asked a generation or two ago. In the chapters that follow I will attempt to address – explicitly or implicitly – these questions and many more. But before moving in that direction I want to address an overriding concern that will help put this whole project into context.

Extended adolescence

In his book *Childhood and Society*, Erik Erikson reveals that many primitive cultures allowed their young people a period of experimenting with freedom. This was at the end of their childhood but before they got married and began to shoulder the responsibilities of adulthood. In bringing our attention to this practice Erikson was suggesting that humans need such a period, that it is part of growing up. But it is time, I believe, to have a good look at what our society is not providing in terms of the passage from childhood to adulthood.

· · · · · · · · · ·

It's a sobering fact that when Mozart was my age
he had already been dead for two years.

Tom Lehrer

· · · · · · · · · ·

Some of you reading these lines may be thinking that I am directing this book towards young people. But I am well aware that people picking up a book about relationships may be anywhere from mid-teens to forty and up. The period of passage between coming out of childhood and becoming a full-fledged adult, engaged in raising a family, has been extended almost interminably. Of course, some people stay in post-secondary education much longer than others. Some take a long time to settle into or find an occupation. Some take a long time to leave home; some leave and then come back to their family home after meeting with a setback or a change in plans. But probably the most crucial aspect of this period of passage is the finding of a mate and committing oneself to living, and raising a family, with that person. Why is it taking so much longer for most people to take this crucial life step?

Collective adolescence

· · · · · · · · · ·

Unlike most other species, we are not biologically
programmed to know what to do;
rather, we are an experiment in free choice.
This leaves us with enormous potential, powerful egotism,
and tremendous anxiety –
a syndrome that is recognizably adolescent.

Elisabet Sahtouris

· · · · · · · · · ·

There is a parallel between the development of an individual and the development of human society. Just as an individual goes through stages of growth, so too does society. Looking at human society as a whole, we can see that we have been going through a period of collective adolescence. Adolescence has been characterized in many ways, most of them tending to be negative. But it need not be so. Adolescence tends to be an experimental period where new limits and powers are tested, albeit sometimes very recklessly. Adolescents are often accused of not seeing reality, of being too idealistic. I like the idealism of young people. It shows a willingness to see the world in another light and to question the problematic world they are inheriting. New ideas and orientations are tried out, often with a disdain for the restraints earlier generations learned while growing up.

These positive and negative aspects of adolescence are all observable when we look at the world as a whole. Competitiveness, impetuosity, human passions, wanting it all, lack of respect for material resources, 'strutting our stuff', looking for attention, winning at all costs, and, as psychiatrist H. B. Danesh has phrased it, 'an intense preoccupation with power, pleasure, and love', are all aspects of an unresolved, prolonged adolescence which is dogging the world as a whole. But there are signs of growing collective maturity, though these have not yet become our prevalent orientation. Signs of our collective coming of age can be seen in the push to resolve conflicts peacefully, in a growing recognition of the need to respect all life and physical resources, in more cooperation in decision making with a goal of consensus, in the increased consciousness that we are living in a global village, that our destinies are all connected and that there is nowhere to go to escape. When these orientations become part and parcel of our global society, then we can say that we are truly coming of age. But, clearly, we have not yet arrived.

Delaying our coming of age

The common aspect of adolescence that I want to focus on here is a reluctance to move on. Perhaps the greater wisdom of early societies in allowing for a period of relative freedom before becoming adult lay in the fact that the period always had a definable and expected end. It may be because we are collectively experiencing our period of adolescence but have not yet found our way through it, that the period of individual adolescence has come to be drawn out. What is problematic in living so long in the limbo of adolescence is that we start to accept it as reality. It can be fun to explore without end but, in the end, we are left feeling estranged and unfulfilled. Moreover, when our adolescent period is extended too long we tend to lose sight of the fact that there is a mature period towards which we should be building. We may start to think that limbo is our reality and stop believing in a mature reality in which we all play a clearly defined role. We lose awareness of what adulthood entails, or we pick and choose aspects of it that are more comfortable to us but leave other aspects out of the picture.

· · · · · · · · · ·

We go round and round and round in the circle game.
Joni Mitchell

· · · · · · · · · ·

Without a clear end in sight, left to our own devices, most of us tend to get stuck and confused. We start out excited, experiencing the thrills of falling in love. Even just the anticipation of falling in love can carry us forward for a time. After a while you begin to realize that most of the experience is hurtful. Great expectations crumble into dark depression. Multiple hurts engender pessimism. Seriousness transforms into game playing. Moral fortitude relaxes into social conformity. Confidence transmutes into self-doubt. We start to realize that almost everyone is falling in and out of relationships with no real purpose and the process seems to be going around in circles rather than yielding useful lessons.

A guide for the perplexed

I am writing this book not as a quick fix to the relationship woes that are benumbing our society, or as a handbook for romance, but to offer an integrated vision that encompasses our spiritual yearnings and can lead us toward a new and rewarding way of developing relationships and – in the process – get to know ourselves in a profound way. But spiritual ambitions do not necessarily lead us to success in relationships. Those who have turned toward spirituality as a way out of the confusion of our times have not often found a way of integrating their spiritual orientation with the finding of a partner. Some consider having a partner as too worldly and have even turned to celibacy as means of escaping the gross and mindless ways that characterize many of our social patterns. Others yield to the natural human impulse to look for a partner but, like most of the rest, are still experimenting and still getting hurt.

• • • • • • • • • •

Ignorance gives one a large range of probabilities.

George Eliot

• • • • • • • • • •

This book is intended as a guide toward helping us arrive at place of clarity, where we see how the psychologically unconscious and spiritually conscious design can be integrated in the most intimate coming together of a man and a woman. You don't have to be spiritually oriented or psychologically informed to appreciate this book, though I hope when you see how understanding our psychological and spiritual nature can bring clarity to the task of finding a partner, you may find yourself growing in appreciation of these aspects of our reality. However, I should forewarn all readers that much of what is put forward will present a challenge.

The ideas in this book point towards a model which our society hasn't arrived at yet. Your orientations and ways of doing things, your own idiosyncratic places of arrival, may be at variance with the counsels this book contains. You may have invested yourself in a relationship, or a way of approaching relationships, which runs counter to what is put forward in the chapters that follow. I have myself taken a long road to uncovering the understandings I am attempting to convey. I have experienced much of the confusion and hurt that is alluded to here – as well as been a source of hurt. Although it may not seem so at times, I have sympathy for all the individuals who struggle – often in great earnestness – to find their way and invent their own solutions in a world that has not yet found a model for courtship which can embrace the new age we are living in. I am offering a broad, integrating view of courtship which, I hope, fits the greater purpose for which we were all created. Take your time with it. If you find the theoretical parts – especially the first chapter – hard to digest, I recommend that you get what you can out of it and move on, for the ideas it contains will be referred to later in the book in more practical ways and you may find you can put the pieces together then.

• • • • • • • • • •

I used to wake up at 4 a.m. and start sneezing,
sometimes for five hours.
I tried to find out what sort of allergy I had
but finally came to the conclusion
that it must be an allergy to consciousness.

James Thurber

• • • • • • • • • •

But putting the pieces together is just part of the challenge. Waking up to areas of our lives that have been neglected or even left untouched is probably the greatest challenge. Sometimes we tend to disregard something new or different because of prejudice; sometimes because it makes us uncomfortable. Society pushes and pulls us in different directions and we all find a way to survive, but often our mechanisms of survival keep us from moving forward in a healthy way. If we are ever going to live in happy partnership with another, we will have to develop in ways that are unsuspected, but nonetheless enriching. Much of the content of this book is an invitation to begin doing this in preparation for such a partnership, an invitation to consciousness.

1

Knowing Ourselves

How can I say anything about you, whom I most probably have not even met? Well, there is actually quite a lot. No matter who you may be, we share our humanity and that means we have much in common. Beyond this huge shared heritage, however, you have traits, propensities and potentials that are completely unique. Still, as a fellow human being, and perhaps also because I am a psychologist who has come to know many others through that unique kind of relationship that therapists develop with their clients, I can share some insights on how we can come to know more about our own selves, both in terms of our uniqueness and in terms of what it means to be a human being.

But why would I want to discuss who we are as humans, what our purpose is and how we can pursue a deeper understanding of our own uniqueness? What does any of this have to do with finding a marriage partner? Let me start by quoting something I read on a refrigerator magnet (don't worry, at least some of my sources will be more scholarly than this): 'Some people make things happen; some people watch things happen; some people wonder "What happened?"' Though I like this statement, I would have added to the beginning, 'Some people make good things happen.'

What does this have to do with finding a marriage partner? Well, it is easy to go through life having an 'I' – we all have one – but we stand in danger of wasting our precious time here just watching what other people do or being occupied with other people's schemes. This is especially true in this age of TV and computer screens. Perhaps worse, we run the risk of feeling a perpetual victim of circumstances. Even if we are 'doers', if we do not know who we are and what we are here for, we run the risk of doing things of little real value or even things that are destructive. Perhaps this is why Socrates said, 'The unexamined life is not worth living.'

· · · · · · · · · ·

A moment's reflection
is preferable to seventy-five years of pious worship.

The Báb

· · · · · · · · · ·

If we don't take the time to examine this 'I' which just sort of exists in the background of everything we do, how can we begin to address life's major challenges, or even to recognize what the major challenges are? Millions of people fall in love, get married, have children, and then later ask the question 'What happened?' or, 'Who is this?' or, 'Why am I in this marriage?' Although we can never know completely who we are, and even though marriage itself is, as we shall see, potentially one of the best vehicles for learning more about ourselves, we still stand a better chance of moving in a healthy direction by gaining self-insight early in the game. It is certainly better to ask the difficult questions now than to wonder 'What happened?' later on.

In examining these questions and others, I will not just draw on my own experience, or lessons from psychology or philosophy. I will draw from my understanding of those paradigmatic individuals whose teachings have most deeply influenced the lives of the greatest number of people, i.e. the founders of the great world religions. The most recent of these, Bahá'u'lláh, is the founder of my own religion, the Bahá'í Faith, and I would not be fair to you if, in addressing these most significant of issues, I did not acknowledge this source which most significantly influences the thoughts I will be sharing with you.

•••••••••

[T]he faith of no man can be conditioned by any one except himself.

Bahá'u'lláh

•••••••••

In acknowledging this, however, I want to say 'Watch out!' Don't let your biases, whether they be against religion – or against this particular religion – turn you off. I am not trying to convert anyone, but just share, here and there, what I regard as important or useful insights gained from my own religion. I also want to say 'Watch out!' because, unless I actually include quotations from the Bahá'í writings, what I say is just my personal interpretation or understanding of spiritual reality and does not represent any official view. Now, back to the questions. Let me begin by making some points about who we humans are and what it is that makes us unique.

Human beings

1.   *We are culture creatures*

More than any other creature, we are dependent on our caregivers to bring us up, nurture, train, and teach us. And this upbringing takes place in an environment of human culture, an environment which is far more significant to us, as humans, than our natural environment. I am not saying that our natural environment is not important, of course it is, and we must learn to care for and relate to it well, or our very survival will be in jeopardy. But it is our human cultural environment which most affects us.

In the process of growing up we are introduced to new possibilities of being; we are trained in new skills. Interestingly, this process of 'enculturation' or socialization is also limiting. We learn these habits and not those; we learn this language and not that; we develop a set of values akin to those of our parents and our society, not those of other adults or other societies. Although, as we shall see, we have an ever-present capacity to move beyond our cultural heritage and to act contrary to the norms of our family or society, we are – to a much larger extent than most of us appreciate – 'stamped' by our culture and its norms. The 'accident' of our being born to our parents and not to other parents, or to our culture and not to another, has a momentous – though not totally binding – influence on who we become.

2.   We are culture creators

Although we always to some degree bear the stamp of the family and culture we are raised in, we also all of us to some extent affect the movement of our family and culture. This is most obviously the case in the cultural figures of each age. Writers, political leaders, famous personalities – these can have a significant influence on millions of people and can even bring about change in our core cultural ideologies, affecting generations to come. But what each person who lives within a culture does with his or her life, when added together with what others do, constitutes what culture is at any moment. We all play our part. The actions or words of one affect another, who in turn affects others. Our actions have a ripple effect and the complex intermingling of these ripples emerge as the complete cultural picture at any given time.

• • • • • • • • • •

The injury of one shall be considered the injury of all;
the comfort of each, the comfort of all;
the honour of one, the honour of all.

'Abdu'l-Bahá

• • • • • • • • • •

It has been said that a single butterfly flapping its wings just once has to have some effect, however minuscule, on the weather everywhere on the planet. In the same way, all individuals, to a greater and lesser extent, are culture movers. Thus, culture is an ongoing process which affects us all but is also to some degree influenced by us. This is most clearly seen in the family – which is a mini-culture. Our family significantly influences us, while each member of the family significantly influences the whole, even those who are 'passive'.

3. *We are the crown of creation*

As humans, we are the apex of all known creation. Nothing yet discovered in the universe even remotely approaches the human being in complexity, intelligence, creativity and all other significant measures. Acknowledging this is not an exercise in self-aggrandizement. Nor does it fly in the face of what many of us feel – that we humans are making a great mess of things. There is no question that we can do things nothing else in the universe is capable of doing. Even many of the bad things we do are unfortunate examples of our prowess at work when we are not guided aright. Our place among creatures is of the highest rank and we cannot escape this aspect of our destiny. It is better to acknowledge this and to look the responsibility it entails straight in the eye. As we shall see, taking responsibility is crucial to a happy marriage. Being responsible and finding a responsible partner is far more productive of happiness and welfare than the seductions we fall into when we live a life unconscious of our high destiny.

In marriage, as in life, we need to hold onto an awareness of the dignity of our station, as well as that of our spouse. We, as humans, have so much more than animals in terms of consciousness – the ability to reflect, to create, to solve problems and to use our higher intelligence – that it is a mistake to think of ourselves as animals, or even animals with higher intelligence. True, we have bodies with biological similarities to animals and we can also, unfortunately, fall into animalistic behaviour. But the human order so far transcends the animal that it is misleading to think of ourselves as animals. Animals also have many biological similarities to plants, but we do not call them plants or plants that move. The difference between a human and an animal is far greater than what distinguishes an animal from a plant. And as humans we even have the capacity to transcend ourselves.

4.   *We are transcended*

· · · · · · · · · ·

The human mind is a great and wondrous thing.
Unfortunately, it did not come with any instructions.

Kurt Vonnegut

· · · · · · · · · ·

To say we are transcended sounds somehow religious and it is true that all the great religions have taught this in one way or another. But, more to the point, it is an existential fact. Every aspect of who we are, including all our thoughts and actions, is encompassed. A fact of human existence is that we work within boundaries. While these boundaries can be stretched and extended, there is always a 'beyond the boundary'. What is beyond the boundary today may be within it tomorrow but there will still be a boundary tomorrow, beyond which lies the ever mysterious infinite which will never be encompassed or grasped.

   In our day-to-day lives we do not think much about what is beyond us. We usually confine our thinking to that which exists comfortably for us within the sphere of what we know well. But if we were to push the boundaries of what we know, even of what is known through our sciences, we would find a limit – questions about which even the most erudite mind cannot come up with an answer. What is not known surrounds us like an abyss that can be frightening to contemplate. It is like death, which ever encompasses our life and is for most of us too frightening to really think about seriously and about which our conscious minds usually live with in a kind of state of denial. This is the essence of what existential philosophers have uncovered, but it is not a very comforting insight into the human condition. Yet Bahá'u'lláh says '... this confession of helplessness which every mature mind is eventually impelled to make ... is in itself, the acme of human understanding.' Looking beyond our boundaries is the beginning of discovery, both in science and in our spiritual life.

· · · · · · · · · ·

... it is from weakness unknown, but perhaps suspected,
as in some parts of the world you suspect a deadly snake in
every bush
– from weakness that may lie hidden,
watched or unwatched, prayed against or manfully scorned,
repressed or maybe ignored more than half a lifetime,
not one of us is safe.

Joseph Conrad

· · · · · · · · · ·

Perhaps because we humans stand at the apex of creation we are prone to arrogance, to exalt in our 'I', but recognition of the fact that we are transcended is conducive to humility. We properly feel small and humble when we really contemplate the universe as a whole and the process of creation that has led to the human creature, the infinitely small point in time and space which our lives occupy. Although this recognition is an imposition on our egos, it is a sign of maturity to be able to access this perspective. Our egos are a huge problem in marriage. They seem either to get bruised or enlarged in our personal relationships and neither is healthy. Remembering that we are always transcended helps us to realize that we are all of us always in the process of becoming, swimming in an infinite sea where feelings of inferiority or superiority are two sides of the same coin, the weight of which always serves to pull us down.

Marriage is a good example of the truth of our being tran-scended and of our ultimate vulnerability. When we fall in love, we feel the power of love and may believe, in all certainty, that we have found the one of our dreams and that our love can conquer all. But as the dynamics of the relationship shift and move into another phase (lovers can never imagine this and pay no attention to the voice of experience which says it always happens) we discover that our partner has his or her own will. Our partner, we come to recognize at some point, may very well choose to do something in exact opposition to us. The one we have based much of our existence on may even, after all, leave us, and we are ultimately powerless to prevent this. The reality surrounding our marriage, our dreams, our comforts, may all just collapse around us. This is a fact our egos would like to deny; in fact, our egos run the gamut from giving in, to aggressively controlling the other, all unconsciously to protect their fragility. It is much healthier to acknowledge the reality of our fragility and not take the marriage for granted, because the marriage that is taken for granted is the one most likely to collapse, just as the life which is taken for granted is the one most likely to be unfulfilled.

5.　*We are potential*

* * * * * * * * * *

Regard man as a mine rich in gems of inestimable value.
Education can, alone,
cause it to reveal its treasures . . .

Bahá'u'lláh

* * * * * * * * * *

Who we are and what we are to become is never set. From the moment of our conception to the moment of our death, we live with a large potential which is not – cannot – be fully tapped. Although we have a genetic inheritance and each of us has a unique collection of capacities, the self that we can be is never fully realized. The genius that was Einstein, for example, would never have blossomed if certain conditions for its development had not been provided, but we cannot say that even his potential was ever even close to being fully tapped.

Even our own self, or sense of self, does not come into being without human stimulus. There are cases where human children have apparently been reared by animals, and they did not develop the qualities of humans. In fact, the primary stimulus for the development of self, and our potential, is in our relationships with others. These others may be teachers, thinkers, writers and so forth, but contact with **any** other has some impact on what we become. In fact, close encounters with very different others who may just be outwardly 'regular' people may, in fact, be a great stimulus to our development. This is one of the reasons marriage is so enriching, because we develop an intimate relationship with someone of a different sex, from a different family, and hopefully maintain that relationship over a long period of time. This stimulates our development of self in ways that are hard to replace.

6.   *We have a shadow self*

Most of us realize that we are not all that we appear to be. We all have thoughts and fantasies that we do not share with others, often because we are too embarrassed or ashamed to talk about them. Because we have such secret thoughts, it doesn't take much to realize that others have them too. Thus we recognize the psychological truth that people have a kind of public face and a private one. Carl Jung called our public face our persona, or mask.

• • • • • • • • • •

. . . mortal man is prone to err, and is ignorant of the mysteries
that lie enfolded within him . . .

Bahá'u'lláh

• • • • • • • • • •

But there is also a side of ourselves which, strange as it may sound, we hide from ourselves. Freud termed this our unconscious, while Jung used the phrase 'shadow self'. Whatever, many psychologists believe that the unconscious propensities that lie beneath the surface of our awareness are akin to that more massive portion of an iceberg which is hidden beneath the surface of the water it floats in. In this view, what we do and how we behave is governed more by this hidden, unknown aspect of our being, or shadow self, than by what we are conscious of.

Most readers, when they encounter what psychologists or psychiatrists have to say about these dark, buried areas of our being, react with dismay or disbelief. Can it be that we have, all of us, dark and morbid fears and wishes lurking somewhere within us? This seems, especially at first sight, to be a whole other world to us, one which we do not have a part in. While Freud and some of his followers may be justifiably criticized for overemphasizing this seemingly negative aspect of humans, or for being overzealous in their theorizing, there is little doubt we have a shadow self. But where does our shadow self come from? I will not go into depth here, but a brief picture of our early socialization will help us to understand this a little more clearly.

Despite what many Christian theologians have referred to as original sin, we come, all of us, into this world in a state of innocence, without sin or any knowledge of sin. However, our biological or animal side has urges, appetites and desires which do not always fall into accord with the demands of human society or our moral beliefs. A mother may send her child out to play and find, an hour later, that the child has come back in treading mud on her expensive carpet, dirty from head to toe. In her horror at seeing this little creature she had sent out with perfectly clean clothes, the mother may deride and scold the child severely, especially if she has already had a hard day. The child, who may have just had a supremely good time playing in the mud, is equally dismayed: coming from the height of pleasure, he or she is now being received as some kind of creature from hell. In time the child will learn its lesson and substitute its ability to find spontaneous pleasure in playing in the mud for hating dirt as much as the mother does. In the process, in addition to learning the virtue of cleanliness, the child may well have buried an aspect of itself which is related to these incidents; this could be an unconscious negative association with being in nature, or perhaps an unconscious guilt in having fun or expressing joy. In other words, the always difficult process of socialization contributes to the formation of our shadow self in some way or other.

• • • • • • • • • •

Some things my mom taught me:
My mother taught me **to appreciate a job well done**.
'If you're going to kill each other, do it outside –
I just finished cleaning!'
My mother taught me about **religion**.
'You better pray that will come out of the carpet.'
My mother taught me **logic**.
'Because I said so, that's why.'
My mother taught me **logic, part 2**.
'If you fall out of that swing and break your neck,
you're not going to the store with me.'
My mother taught me **foresight**.
'Make sure you wear clean underwear,
in case you're in an accident.'
My mother taught me **irony**.
'Keep crying and I'll give you something to cry about.'
My mother taught me **about contortionism**.
'Will you look at the dirt on the back of your neck!'
My mother taught me **about hypocrisy**.
'If I've told you once, I've told you a million times –
don't exaggerate!'
My mother taught me **the circle of life**.
'I brought you into this world, and I can take you out.'
Anonymous

• • • • • • • • • •

21

Becoming human, and the process of socialization which this necessarily entails, is much more complex and trying than we realize, and much of the frustration and confusion remains buried, becoming part of our shadow self. This becomes a kind of blind spot in our psyches which we carry into all our adult relationships. The more crucial the relationship – and, of course, marriage is probably the most crucial – the more likely our shadow self will be brought to the surface. When the shadow self does come to the surface it seems to come out of nowhere, both for us and our unsuspecting partner, and we usually behave in a manner all out of proportion to the stresses involved that somehow caused it to surface. Thus, recognizing our shadow self and realizing that we all have one is a helpful antecedent to finding a partner and getting married.

7.   We choose

Most people who are reading this will have heard of the debate about 'nature versus nurture'. This is the long-standing argument about whether who we are is more a result of our genetic make up (nature) or whether our personality is more a result of our upbringing and environmental factors (nurture). Earlier in this chapter when we talked about unconscious forces and socialization, we were exploring social factors or nurture. In other sections (for example, when describing human uniqueness) the presumption has usually been that these aspects of our being human have to do with our genetic make-up. But these two factors of nature and nurture, and even the way they interact, fall short of answering the question of who, really, we humans are. Psychologist Alfred Adler has asserted that a far more significant aspect of our selves is our ability to set goals and make choices. He called this the 'Third Force'.

• • • • • • • • • •

Man is My mystery, and I am his mystery.

Muhammad

• • • • • • • • • •

To appreciate this we have to pull ourselves out of the incomplete view of the universe that we may have developed as a part of our school education – that is, the misleading picture that the universe and everything in it is a kind of mechanism. Human beings, from this point of view, are biological mechanisms – very complex, but essentially mechanistic. A mechanism can be understood and its actions predicted, if we are able to become aware of all its constituents and how the various forces work upon these constituents. The movement of a billiard ball, to take a fairly simple example, can be predicted if we know about the material makeup of the ball and the energy and direction of another ball running into it. But human beings are different. Even if we could know all the complex factors – genetic and environmental – that operate on a human (and much of psychology tries to uncover and understand these factors), we cannot begin to say we have fully understood who that person is or what he or she will do at any given moment. We need, ultimately, to know what that person's intention is. Adler was aware that many if not most of our goals are unconscious, but that we all have the potential at any moment to choose for ourselves a direction which may contradict all antecedents or predicted courses. Humans, according to Adler, are best understood when we understand their goals and intentions – unconscious or conscious – and their capacity to choose a path of their own design.

We do not know exactly when the faculty which enables us to make conscious choice comes into play, but it is most certainly one of the most momentous developments in our individual and collective history. The domain of human intention is rightfully personal. All previous development and evolution finds its consummation in this development. This unique capacity of humans is such a magnificent gift that it can become a source of arrogance and often becomes our worst enemy. It is our sovereign ground, given to us by our Creator. It is ours to use or abuse. Unfortunately, we seem to have a massive predilection to abuse it and go off in directions which are unhealthy, destructive, and heedless of our high station.

• • • • • • • • • •

*For every one of you his paramount duty is to choose for himself
that on which no other may infringe
and none usurp from him.*

Bahá'u'lláh

• • • • • • • • • •

One of the most significant steps in developing self-knowledge happens when we awaken to our ability to make choices and to take conscious responsibility for them. This entails coming to terms with the wounds of our past and to develop a positive, forward-looking orientation to our future possibilities. Taking responsibility for our ability to choose our actions, to get past blame and resentment, can awaken in us a healthy respect for our place in the universe and to discover our purpose for being here.

8.   *We are moral creatures*

One consequence of our being able to choose is that we become moral creatures. This is also tied to our being social creatures. Many animals are social in nature, and nature as a whole works in a 'community' manner whereby the whole and its parts work to maintain a healthy homeostasis. But in nature, and with social animals which are a part of nature, none of this is done consciously. There is no choice involved. We humans, who do have a choice, and who live in societies, have to learn how to behave – that is, to make moral choices – in order to get along.

• • • • • • • • • •

Man's social life is essentially a moral affair.

John Shotter

• • • • • • • • • •

Morality has a deeply personal dimension as well as a profoundly social one. The latter evolves over centuries and is passed on through socialization. The former emerges for each individual as soon as we awaken to our ability to make choices. This is one way in which we are both culture creatures and culture creators. A mature human is one who is awake to both dimensions of morality and seeks to develop a high level of personal morality and to contribute to the ongoing development of the social order. The family is a workshop for developing both the personal and social dimensions of our morality, making moral maturity an essential component of a healthy marriage.

9.   We are souls

To say we are souls brings us again clearly into the domain of the religious. In the Bahá'í teachings we are taught that our soul is our essence. The soul is also potential, but its potential is of a spiritual sort. The soul is all the good that we can become, all the virtues such as honesty, integrity, creativity, perseverance, love, justice, forgiveness, and joyfulness. The soul comes to the fore when we are in touch with our true purpose, and in the Bahá'í writings we are told that it is the soul that has the capacity to recognize its Creator.

Our soul lives in association with our body while our body lives, but being a spiritual entity, does not die when our body dies. Our soul, in this life, can be seen as a kind of counterbalance to our ego. Somehow we have to develop an ego to become a creature capable of choice, yet the ego – spiritually speaking – becomes problematic. We often choose to pursue our appetite for things which have nothing to do with our purpose in this world. Because of the unique capacities we have as humans, when we direct our wills toward our animal appetites we become much worse than animals. This is because we are created for a spiritual purpose. Although chasing the things of this world gives no deep satisfaction, it may, nevertheless, **feel** good. Thus our ego can endlessly mislead us and become compulsively entwined with meaningless pursuits. Our soul, on the other hand, responds to spiritual stimulation. Our soul exalts in fulfilling a higher purpose and the feeling of deep satisfaction is the voice of the soul. When we learn to listen to this voice the persistent call of our ego can for these moments be silenced. In these moments we are finding our way.

• • • • • • • • • •

The troubles of this world pass, and what we have left is what we have made of our souls.

On behalf of Shoghi Effendi

• • • • • • • • • •

Marriage, because it is a spiritual and a physical coming together, will test and hone all of our capacities. While there is an obvious strong material component to marriage, the material demands ultimately serve as occasions for spiritual growth. It is profoundly significant that in the Bahá'í writings we are counselled to marry, to have an occupation, to make money and spend it on the welfare of our family, to enjoy sexual relations with our spouse, to have a home. All of these are practical, material, and – one could say – worldly pursuits, but they are not to be done for the glorification of our egos. They are responsibilities we are counselled to take on and, in the process, if we honour our souls, they accrue to our spiritual development. Both our own and our spouse's spiritual development **and** our souls' relationship with each other continue after our life in this world has ended.

10. *We are in search of our Creator*

• • • • • • • • • •

If logic tells you that life is a meaningless accident, don't give up on life. Give up on logic.

Shira Milgrom

• • • • • • • • • •

From a scientific point of view, our creation is a truly amazing phenomenon. From a single supercharged point believed to be the 'seed' of the whole universe, there emerged, after the spectacular release of this energy, pre-atomic particles which were organized into pre-galactic formations. When atoms formed they coalesced, producing stars which formed galactic patterns. Stars exploded, others formed from the now greater diversity of atomic material. Eventually, at least in our very, very small corner of this huge process, planets which were part of the debris of an exploded star stepped into file to circle around one of the billions of stars in this galaxy and, at least on this planet, through a favourable confluence of factors, molecules formed, grew in complexity, and eventually became primitive life forms which themselves played their part in transforming the climate of this planet so that life forms became more complex until from this process emerged humans.

Humans, as we have already discussed, stand at the pinnacle of this amazing process wherein energy manifests itself in ever more diverse and complex ways. Remarkably, humans – and only humans – have the ability, especially now, to look back upon this whole process and ask the question 'Why?' This, of course, is not a question that science seeks to answer, nor can it. The quest of science is to understand the dynamics at play. But humans have a sense of purpose. Science itself is impelled by a sense of purpose. So we ask ourselves, if the forces of this unfolding universe eventuated in a creature – the human – which has a sense of purpose and is best understood by learning what its intentions are, then doesn't the 'seed' of our universe have a creative purpose? This is the heart of the quest of our soul, which seeks the pattern

· · · · · · · · · ·

In this journey the seeker reacheth a stage wherein he seeth all
created things
wandering distracted
in search of the Friend.

Bahá'u'lláh

· · · · · · · · · ·

that connects, and its own part in that pattern, that pattern which is the Soul, if you will, of the Universe.

The path to self-discovery

The above points are really just an outline of who we are and what we are about. The uniqueness of every individual requires of us that we seek out truth, search for our creator's will for us, reflect upon our life's purpose and awaken to our potential. Since we are social creatures, learning to live in true community is part of our quest and an essential aspect of the process of coming to know ourselves. Marriage is the foundation of community, and both our path to finding a partner and marriage itself are intimately linked to our individual spiritual destiny. Thus, the chapters that follow will also lead us into further elucidation about who we are. Later, after we have laid the groundwork for the development of a healthy marriage, we will return to the subject of self-knowledge and see how all this ties together.

2

Knowing the Other:
Differences between Men and Women

Some readers may have found the previous chapter pretty hard going. We humans are complex creatures, and acquiring a deep understanding of ourselves is no easy task. Gaining an under-standing of the opposite sex can be even more daunting. Fortunately, members of the opposite sex are still human (though we may sometimes feel otherwise) and we can apply much of what we understand about ourselves to them as well. The points made in the previous chapter apply to humans in general; what we will explore now are some of the important differences between male humans and female humans, for it is the two that make the mix we know as marriage.

Boys and girls

· · · · · · · · · ·

Boy, n.: A noise with dirt on it.

Internet graffiti

· · · · · · · · · ·

Interestingly, even when boys and girls grow up together, they tend to grow into different worlds. To some degree the different innate propensities of boys and girls move us in different directions. At the same time, our agents of socialization tend to accent and enhance these differences, perhaps even introducing differences that are not innate at all. In addition, there is a period when boys and girls tend to pull apart of their own accord, creating their own more or less exclusive gender 'clubs', establishing and proclaiming their gender distinctiveness, each in their own peculiar fashion.

These are, of course, parallel worlds which are being created, both of which exist – or, more correctly, co-exist – within one society. Sometimes, in some school systems for example, boys and girls are physically separated, highlighting the 'otherness' of sex, but even in co-educational systems males and females become somehow separate domains akin to separate societies. We must remember that, as humans, we are quite capable of creating boundaries in our minds that can be just as powerful and real as physical boundaries. As girls and boys start to see themselves as inhabiting different universes, they start, in a way, to do just that.

Our distinctiveness in terms of gender comes partly from a deep unconscious well. As mentioned in Chapter 1, Carl Jung referred to our buried unconsciousness as our shadow self. Later in his career Jung refined this concept. This was when he came to see that the content of the shadow self of men was significantly different from that of women. At this point, Jung gave the shadow self of men and women different names: 'anima', for men and 'animus', for women. Jung's earlier form-ulations regarding the shadow self still have relevance: not all that lurks below the surface can be understood in terms of the anima or animus. But these later characterizations can help us in forming a base from which we can begin to understand important differences between men and women, an under-standing that in turn, will help us form a clearer picture of the challenges of marriage.

Men

· · · · · · · · · ·

Man is the missing link between the ape and the human being.

Feminist graffiti

· · · · · · · · · ·

Men, according to Jung, no matter how outwardly masculine, have a feminine side. This feminine side of a man's nature, through the course of socialization, comes to be buried or repressed. It is this repressed feminine aspect of males which Jung termed the anima. One example of the anima can be seen in the expression of feelings. Generally, women are more in touch with their feelings and more able to express their feelings outwardly. Men, on the other hand, are more likely to be unaware of the diverse range of feelings they have – less able to identify and express them. It is not that men do not have feelings. But men usually have less ability to identify their feelings. Also, in the course of our upbringing, we are often taught (consciously or unconsciously) to associate a certain amount of shame with these feelings.

Men's inhibition with respect to feelings is a significant aspect of our psychological development. Somehow, as men, we usually internalize the message that we must be 'strong' – in 'control' – and this is translated – even implicitly intended – to mean not to feel sadness, tenderness, humiliation, embarrassment, hurt, in fact, a whole range of emotions which are part of our self but become cut off from our sense of self. Typically, when these sensitivities are touched, men tend to react – but not with a fluid and open expression or even awareness of these feelings. Rather, we tend to use anger – either the cold or hot variety – to cover the whole range of feelings which may be touched in us.

While reacting with anger or denial with respect to our feelings is the more socially sanctioned way of being male, it is not healthy. One of the reasons males are more inclined to consume alcohol, and more prone to alcoholism, is so that this unhealthy bottling up of a whole range of feelings can have some release, even if not a very conscious one. Under the influence of alcohol, men often become very sentimental, even if they do not remember it the next day. Of course, this is not a healthy release of emotions. The man who gets drunk may feel somewhat less uptight the next day, but at a cost to his physical health and well-being. Also, he will not have learned anything more about himself and will go on perpetuating the same reality in his daily life that brought him to wanting to get drunk in the first place.

Most men tend to be out of touch with their female side. The more extreme type of this has come to be called 'macho', and it is often the bravado of the macho male that puts itself forward as being a real man. Being macho is not what it appears on the surface, rather it is a kind of lie, a fear of revealing or exploring our fuller self. In fact, being a macho male has other consequences, even biological ones. Contrary to popular understanding, studies done on 'macho' males have revealed that they tend to have lower fertility rates than other men and to have hormonal imbalances. The macho male is not a healthy model, but rather one that is more extremely cut off from an important side of itself. Understanding this can at least help us males to seek out more healthy role models and begin to come to terms with our anima, the female aspect of our self, which we have to some degree buried. This is an important extension of self-knowledge and self-development.

But this recognition of the anima and how its suppression manifests itself psychologically is important for females as well. As we will see in chapter 4 on attraction, women are most often attracted to men who manifest these symptoms of partial self. In fact, this kind of blind reaction in women is often a manifestation of their own lack of being in touch with their shadow self, in this case their animus or masculine side, and this is what we will examine next.

Women

One aspect of women which tends to get suppressed in the process of socialization is the ability to be competent outside the

• • • • • • • • • •

People call me a feminist whenever I express sentiments that
differentiate me from a doormat or a prostitute.

Rebecca West

• • • • • • • • • •

domestic or supportive sphere. Women who do not bring their animus to consciousness may not feel able or inclined to take charge, to assert themselves, to think for themselves and act on their own ideas, especially outside the home. One potentially disastrous consequence of this, socially, is that the world 'out there' is left to the men to organize and take care of. Psychologically, a whole side of women's sense of self fails to develop as long as her animus remains in the shadow. This manifests itself in various ways. In marriage women often feel a lack of purpose and frequently fall prey to depression.

• • • • • • • • • •

I do not wish women to have power over men,
but over themselves.

Mary Wollstonecraft (1797)

• • • • • • • • • •

Women are not only up against the desire of the ego to keep unconscious issues at bay, they are up against the force of a male-dominated society not to 'compete' with men in the social sphere. Of course, women who do take strides to find meaningful vocation outside the home are not doing this to compete, but compete only because that is the way the social order has been constructed by men. More on this later, but for now it is important for us to understand that both the forces of the ego and those of society conspire against women coming to terms with their masculine side. This understanding is crucial to our preparation for marriage. A new standard is emerging in our world and it is critical that our personal development match this new standard. Further, how to do this in a hardened, male-dominated society, without losing their feminine strengths and nature creates a kind of double bind.

· · · · · · · · · ·

All I want is a warm bed and a kind word, and unlimited power.

Ashleigh Brilliant

· · · · · · · · · ·

It is helpful for men to recognize the way a woman's suppression of her animus, or masculine side, reveals itself. Whereas men tend to highlight their feelings of inner insecurity by dominating others, women tend to show their insecurities by immersing themselves in the care of others and negating their own egos. This feeds into the stereotypical male pattern perfectly. A man will see or sense that this is a woman who can be dominated, who will yield to his own ego, that he will be 'safe' with such a woman as his partner. A kind of unconscious contract is drawn up between such partners and becomes the basis for many, many relationships, a most unhealthy base which tends to conspire against the growth of each of them.

· · · · · · · · · ·

I wish men would get more in touch with their feminine side, and become self-destructive.

Betsy Salkind

· · · · · · · · · ·

While both men and women have a shadow self, essential aspects of the shadow self, as we have seen, are different. One very important aspect concerning how these differences are projected into the social world needs to be brought forward here. Although an unexplored, unconscious shadow self is a source of insecurity for both sexes, men tend to compensate for this sense of insecurity by seizing power, asserting themselves and taking control. In other words, men quite understandably fall back on their masculine strengths when their areas of insecurity are breached. But this affects the nature of society itself and this society, in turn, reflects back on the development of all the individuals within it. For this reason, we need to take a more conscious look at the social world we are unconsciously creating.

Towards equality

••••••••••

It's a man's world, and you men can have it.

Katherine Anne Porter

••••••••••

Up to this point we have come to understand that, on a social scale, men's tendency to compensate for the weaknesses they feel by 'taking charge' creates an imbalance in society. This creates a situation in the social world where the **differences** between men and women emerge as **inequalities**. Men, in taking charge in this way, create a society which is, in many ways, a projection of our unwholesome, insecure psychological states. The social world, which is the world we all come to know and experience as 'reality', takes on the hardness, competitiveness, and aggressiveness of the male psyche which is largely out of touch with its anima, its feelings and sense of compassion.

••••••••••

Where a system of oppression has become institutionalized
it is unnecessary for individuals to be oppressive.

Florynce Kennedy

••••••••••

We all internalize the standards of our social world. These are the standards by which we are measured and according to which we measure ourselves. Thus, especially since the male propensity for competitiveness has become a standard for our society, society has become dominated by those who are strongest in the predominantly male characteristics which society extols.

By and large, a male-dominated world is a world in which there are winners and losers. This is a paternalistic society and, outwardly at least, females as a group are cast as losers, a group (not the only group) which is dominated and seen, often unconsciously, as something lesser. This serves the unconscious purpose of the insecure male ego to keep the female under his thumb.

It is important to understand this social context of inequality and its pathological ground. Today there is a shift, a movement away from this pattern and this, in turn, is presenting unique challenges, especially to the institution of marriage. Just as there are inequalities favouring men in the paternalistic system we have inherited, there is also an inequality in the psychological pain experienced as we participate in the inevitable changes that are taking place. Men, in a system moving away from male dominance, are finding it more difficult to adapt to the changes.

· · · · · · · · · ·

When a woman behaves like a man, why doesn't she behave like a nice man?

Edith Evans

· · · · · · · · · ·

Many have come to view the changes taking place as a kind of battle between the sexes. In this view, men, who have had power, are going to have it taken away by women who are gaining power. In the Bahá'í teachings, where one of the fundamental principles is the equality of the sexes, the issue is seen in a different light. The orientation towards power is predominantly a male quality. As we learn to project a more equitable balance of male and female attributes into our society the overall power orientation of our society will shift. For example, when the more female attributes of cooperation and mutual support become part of the fibre of our social structures, we will find ourselves, both men and women, functioning in a more wholesome environment, one where power and control is no longer the name of the game.

Marriage, which up to now has been seen as a kind of victim of the processes of social change toward gender equality is, in the Bahá'í view, the primary institution for transforming society. This must especially apply with respect to the establishment of gender equality. Far from being a battleground of the sexes, marriage ought to ultimately become the means of the masculine and feminine coming together and finding balance in our consciousness and behaviour. Marriage will be the leading force in bringing about a wholesome change in our society when both men and women accept the psychological challenges and advantages it presents. When we enter into marriage with maturity and preparedness, and support each other in the process of the change we know we are to face, the process will result in each gender discovering wholeness. Marriage, in this scenario, becomes an environment that fosters the wholesome development of all its family members and will project itself into society in a way that will help to move that society in a healthy direction.

'Cultural' differences

• • • • • • • • • •

Men and women, women and men. It will never work.

Erika Jones

• • • • • • • • • •

The differences between the anima and the animus, the respective shadow selves of men and women, are the foundation of many other differences. Although some maintain that the sexes do not differ in any significant way, men and women are indeed different in many respects. These differences and the way we handle them are very much like cultural differences. Their source is hotly debated. Men and women have some biological differences and some genetic differences and our physiological propensities may, to some degree, propel us to behave and develop in psychologically different ways. Socialization is, of course, a huge factor in human development and many studies have revealed how differently boys and girls are socialized from earliest infancy, even though the primary socialization agents – mother and father – may be completely unaware of this. In fact, these differences in socialization seem to occur even when the father and mother are trying consciously to do otherwise. It is also being recognized more and more, especially by evolutionary psychologists, that there are very real differences in make-up between the average man and the average woman.

Whatever the origin of gender differences, they are many and varied. While the fact of differences is widely recognized, we cannot see them as absolute or rule-like. It is in this sense that gender differences behave more like cultural differences. Swedes, for example, are different from Spaniards in many ways. Europeans differ probably even more considerably from Africans. Yet we can always find individuals within these societies who do not fit their cultural stereotype. There are Southern Europeans who have quite rigid personal behaviours, who are well organized and who put their work before pleasure, while there are Northern Europeans who are very spontaneous, who do not plan ahead and who are ready to drop their workload at any moment to have a good time. There are, likewise, Africans who spend too much time at the office, who immerse themselves in books and numbers and who cannot sing in tune or dance in rhythm. At the same time, there are Europeans who have the physical grace and open-heartedness we usually associate with Africans. The same overlapping and breaking down of stereo-types occurs with respect to gender differences. With this disclaimer that exceptions to the stereotypes abound, and further, that some are just pure fiction, the following table shows a list of gender differences generated by participants in one of the workshops my wife and I held with a multicultural group of adults, both men and women. The ideas were theirs but I have attempted to line up the items placed at the top of the chart for purposes of comparison:

Gender differences

Woman	Man
pays attention	plans
holds family together	family supporter
merciful	concerned about justice
detail-oriented	whole-oriented
selfless	possessive
influenced by feelings	logical
intuitive	focused on matter
spiritual	physical
communicative	task-oriented
can concentrate on several things at once	separates things into compartments
concerned for others	looks after self first
relationship-oriented	action-oriented
sensitive	loves football
flexible	inflexible
strong	easily injured
persevering	
chatters	
able to stretch herself	
expects tenderness	
extreme	
orderly	
complex	
patient	
faithful	
	concentrates
	can separate work from family

• • • • • • • • • •

Why can't a woman be like a man?

Professor Higgins

• • • • • • • • • •

These kinds of differences, while not universal, are nevertheless significant enough to become the source of conflict and misunderstanding in personal relationships, especially in marriage. The irony is that we are, most of us, programmed to be attracted to the opposite sex, yet being opposite in so many ways becomes the source of battles and frustrations. We pull out our hair at the other and yearn for him or her to be 'like us'.

These differences play themselves out most intensively in marriages, especially after marriages have passed beyond the romantic phase. As such, they may not seem very relevant to couples who are at the stage of courtship. It is worth including them partly just to inform the unwary. However, recognizing gender differences can also help us to build understanding, even at the earlier stages of our relationships.

One example of how gender differences play themselves out in the early stages of relationships has to do with romance itself. Women often have the desire, and even the expectation, that their mate will 'sense' their needs or even anticipate them. It *is* possible for a couple to be so in tune with each other that they can anticipate the other's desires and wants and, of course, it is very gratifying and confirming when this happens. This ability seems to be rarer in men, and if it is present at all it is usually just at the peak of romance when the couple still have not begun to relate to each other as regular human beings. It can also occur much later in a marriage when the couple have developed a truly mature and deep love for one another. There are also some men who have a much better idea of what women appreciate and use this knowledge, and the fact that women love to have their desires anticipated, to manipulate them into sexual relationships when they have no intention of committing themselves in marriage. It is important to know that when this ability manifests itself in the man at an early stage of a relationship, it is not necessarily the sign of 'true' love that women often mistake it to be. Conversely, its lack in a relationship is not necessarily a sign of a lack of love but more likely just an indication that the woman is in the company of, well, a male. While it may be good for a man to cultivate this kind of sixth sense, when he does not it is definitely counterproductive for the woman to bemoan her plight and conclude that her mate does not really love her.

· · · · · · · · · ·

Even if man could understand woman he still wouldn't believe it.

A.W. Brown

· · · · · · · · · ·

Men for their part – and this, too, can happen early in a relationship – are often astonished at how affected women can be by seemingly small things. We react to this in many ways and most of them are not healthy. At these times our gut reaction is something like 'How can she be like this? What more does she want? What is her problem?' or, like Professor Higgins, 'Why can't a women be like us?' Usually we take offence, but in fact there is much that we can learn about ourselves in these moments of frustration, if we can get past our own hurt male egos.

The real difficulties that come in facing gender differences usually need to be confronted in marriage and handled in different stages. As most of this does not pertain to courtship itself, we will not here go into great detail. Rather, we can list the stages in this process to show in large brush strokes what a couple can gain through years of being married. The first stage or two can, to some degree, be accomplished before marriage and the more our eyes are open to these issues and our hearts open to the process, the better it will be for our marriages.

Stages in understanding the opposite sex

1.   Knowledge of differences

The first step is to become aware of the differences between men and women. This is an ongoing process which we have begun to explain already, but much more needs to be done in this area in order for today's marriages to become successful. We should take notice of these differences and strive to be aware of the extent to which we – or our potential spouses – manifest these signs and how much they have to do with being men or women. We should also be careful not to stereotype to the point where we no longer 'see' the other in their individual uniqueness.

2.   Acceptance of differences

· · · · · · · · · ·

The only way to make a husband over according to one's ideas . . . would be to adopt him at an early age, say four.

Mary Roberts Rinehart

· · · · · · · · · ·

The next step, since we can never really mould the other according to our wishes anyway, is to accept the differences – to see them as aspects of femininity or masculinity. An incredible amount of frustration in relationships can be avoided if we can learn to accept that the other is the way he or she is largely because he or she is a he or a she! If a husband is not showing great concern over how his wife feels about something, if he is not inclined to question her or to notice she is not happy about something, it does not mean that he does not love her. Women show love in this way, men have not generally learned this mode of showing love. Conversely, if a wife brings up something she sees needing improving in her husband's behaviour, it does not mean that she is rejecting him as a person. She wants to talk about it, we do not need to take offence and go on a rampage because of our bruised egos.

3. *Learning new ways of being*

A higher goal in this process is to strive to learn from the other. Men have the potential to be more caring and relationship-oriented; women have the capacity to assert themselves in the world and put their ideas forward with confidence. Why not open ourselves to these new possibilities and others, which our mates reveal to us? We have much capacity to develop some of those capacities which seem at first to be gender specific. This is, of course, more easily accomplished if the other does not expect us to change, therein lies the importance of step two. Also, this latter, more advanced development usually takes place over time in a loving marriage. It is one of the priceless fruits of patience and acceptance in a wholesome, long-term relationship. Here, we come to discover the capacity to complete our self, to become whole, to embrace both the female and male within ourselves.

*** *** ***

Much of the content of this chapter may seem to have more to do with marriage itself than with the path to marriage. Yet the knowledge of gender differences and how these differences play themselves out in marriage leads to a more realistic picture of what marriage is. In marriage we are going to have an ongoing intimate encounter with 'the other'. This is at times inevitably painful and trying but, approached with a healthy attitude, incredibly enriching. Because this book has to do with the process of finding a partner and courtship, and not with marital issues, we will not go in any depth here about what to do when encountering differences in a long-term relationship.

Getting to know the opposite sex through groups of friends is helpful as preparation for the challenging path of marriage. Also, it is definitely helpful to our growth to encounter 'the other' in new contexts. For example, it helps us to grow when we develop close bonds with people of different cultures, especially those who are members of a different racial group, and particularly one with which the group we identify with has unresolved difficulties. The reason for this is that our repressed shadow self can be brought to the surface in close encounters with any significantly different 'other', offering opportunities to expand our psychological boundaries and become more aware of who we really are. For this same reason, cross-cultural or cross-racial marriages offer perhaps the most potentially rewarding possibilities. But beware! The challenges of such marriages are also proportionally greater.

We have an intrinsic interest in the opposite sex. Some of this is purely biological, some is a result of the fact that the opposite sex is a different world from our own and we are naturally curious about it. But we also have barriers and fears with respect to this other world. These have to do with our ego boundaries and our resistance to 'the other'. We have suspicions and prejudices and we have primal associations with intimacy and loss which we instinctively know are going to be touched when we allow ourselves to become closely tied into the life of another. Thus, the stakes are inherently high when considering the choice of a partner. Let us now embark on the first stage of encounter, the path of search.

3

The Path of Search

Do not look back in anger, or forward in fear,
but around in awareness.

James Thurber

· · · · · · · · · ·

A question many single people are confronted with is 'Where can I find the person of my choice?' Often, the coming about of a partnership is seen as something that 'just comes when it is supposed to come'. There is, of course, some truth in this, but it is we individuals who choose, after all. This is a responsibility we can work towards with care and diligence.

Like many other important choices we make in life, the choice of a partner, or even the way we approach choosing a partner, needs thorough preparation. We prepare and arrange our lives for everything important. We prepare for our exams by studying, we prepare for our jobs by learning a specific skill. Marriage, and the path towards marriage, also needs preparation, perhaps to an even greater extent since this is one of the most important choices in our lives. Once we have reached the stage where we feel we know ourselves well, are mature and feel ready to get married, we should realize that there are many hazards and difficulties which we are likely to run up against on the path of search. Two of these, which we are bound to encounter because they originate from within us, are delusion and wilfulness.

Delusion and wilfulness

Delusion and wilfulness usually go hand-in-hand. We may, for example, come across someone who we think is perfect (this is the delusion), and we then set out to trap that person at all costs (this is wilfulness). Now, I am not saying we shouldn't picture the possibility that a certain person may make a good partner, nor that we shouldn't take steps to get to know that person better. In fact, what we imagine to be a good partner **needs** to be tested, and this can be a productive use of our will at the early stages. However, using our will to serve our delusion is a sure recipe for disaster or deep disappointment. Let me illustrate this with a couple of real-life examples.

One young man, let's call him Francisco, was very discouraged by the kind of young women he was meeting. They all seemed shallow and reckless. He was serious, a churchgoer, looking for a woman who shared his values. Nothing wrong here. He came to notice that one of the students living in the same dormitory as him – we can call her Maria – went to the same church as he did and this piqued his interest. He took steps to get to know her. To Francisco, Maria seemed different from the others and he became very interested in her. For her part, she didn't reject him but neither was she clearly reciprocating his advances. In a way, her 'cool' attitude enticed him all the more. Up to this point we have so far only witnessed the naivety of Francisco's untested imagination.

Francisco had read a book on positive thinking. From this book he had learned that when you really want something, you should picture it in your mind, be sure of its attainment, and work towards your goal with full effort until it is achieved. He applied what he learned from this book to winning the heart of Maria, sparing no expense, courageously moving forward with full conviction of ultimate success. Some months later he discovered Maria having sexual relations with someone else in his dormitory. Francisco was devastated and severely disappointed.

My second example has similar elements but this time it was a woman who had set her heart on a man who really impressed her. Like Francisco, this woman (we'll call her Ilona) had encountered similar teachings about positive thinking and visualization. In Ilona's case, she had already developed these skills in her work, where she was a tremendously successful salesperson, the top in her area. Perhaps because she had been honing her skills in positive thinking for some years she was more 'successful' in pursuing the man she fully intended to marry. The man, by the way, whom we shall call Istvan, was attractive to many women. Among the steps Ilona took on the path to marry Istvan was to buy herself an expensive new purse and have her initials emblazoned in it. Not her initials as they **were**, but as they **would be** after he had married her (at this point he hardly even knew her!). Ilona eventually got her man, but a very short while after the wedding their marriage was already in deep trouble. After much valiant effort on both parts, the marriage ended in divorce with extremely hurt feelings, especially on her part.

· · · · · · · · · ·

The best things in life aren't things.

Art Buchwald

· · · · · · · · · ·

Both these stories illustrate quite vividly some crucial lessons about the path of search. You will remember from Chapter 1 that we all have a persona, or mask, which is our means of presenting ourselves to the world. This mask can be very enticing but it typically only represents a small part of who we are. People's personas are often most attractive when playing those roles in society for which we have developed considerable skills. The persona of an office manager, for example, may portray competence and power. Others may be attracted when observing him or her in this role, but the persona may not say anything about this person's capacity as a spouse or parent. Similarly, thousands may be attracted to pop singers or actors without having any real idea what they are like as people. One of the reasons Ilona and others were attracted to Istvan was that he was 'in his element' in social situations. But Ilona could not begin to live with him in the more closed intimate climate of marriage. This does not mean that an impressive persona is bad or that it is just some kind of show. Sometimes our persona is just show; sometimes it is an outright distortion of who we are, but often it is also an honest putting forward of ourselves into the public sphere. But in all these cases, there is much more to know about a person than his or her persona and it is our private character which is much more crucial to a marital relationship.

The need to learn about the private character of a potential partner is just one lesson to be learned from the above stories; the other lesson has to do with the investment of our will. This is really a lesson to be learned in life as a whole, but in the highly charged arena of courtship – and given the high stakes of marriage – the lessons are of great significance and are more keenly felt. Let me start by saying that although both the above stories involved the use of techniques of positive thinking I am not making positive thinking the culprit. In fact, I believe in thinking positively myself and sometimes turn to cognitive approaches in my therapy to help my clients see how a negative voice within them can pull them into depression and a sense of helplessness (see later in this chapter). The main point to be gleaned from the above stories, in my view, is that no matter how much we desire something, we need, ultimately, to bow our will to that which encompasses us. We need – at all times, but especially at these times – to find a way of gaining some perspective, so that we can see the other (and ourselves) more clearly. Ironically, we often need to be able to do this at those very times when we often feel most cocksure of our decisions.

Bowing our will to that which encompasses us means connecting to the higher good. Spiritually this means God, and for this, developing the arts of prayer and meditation are indispensable. I will go into this a little later in this chapter. But the higher good can also mean the good of others, the good of society, and the good of ideals which help to build community. For this, gaining the perspective of others can help us to get unblocked from the perils of our own egos.

We are not an island

We have already clarified in Chapter 1 that we are social creatures. Let us now explore this concept in the context of searching for a mate. There are those among us who might be classed as loners. Loners are people who like to keep largely to themselves. Sometimes loners spend time around other people but, if they do, they do not usually let other people in much. They may not share their thoughts and feelings and they may not ask for the opinions of others on personal matters. A loner might turn to a book such as this, but will not usually turn to people for counsel on matters of personal or social concern. Still, even loners usually come around to contemplating finding a partner.

· · · · · · · · · ·

No man is an island but some of us are pretty long peninsulas.

Ashleigh Brilliant

· · · · · · · · · ·

Although loners are often thinkers, the stance of being a loner is not a well-thought-out one. Being a loner is usually a retreat from social reality because social reality can – or already has – been the cause of hurt. It may seem like a sensible stance to retreat from potential hurt but, because we are social creatures, we also have social requirements. We all make some kind of contact with the social world. A loner is someone who strives to minimize this contact. This is not healthy and conspires against success in marriage because marriage is quintessentially a social institution. Marriage brings couples close together, usually results in bringing new family members into the world, members who will play their own social role. This should not be denied, nor retreated from, but soberly acknowledged and faced.

I am bringing this up at this point because at the stage of search the perspective and assistance of others can go a long way in helping us on our path. Now, since the stance of the loner often comes from painful experiences in his or her family of origin, it may not work for the loner to turn to his or her parents for assistance. If not, it is still well worth seeking out healthy substitutes. This goes for all those who, for one reason or another, do not see in their parents the kind of people who would be useful in addressing questions about finding a partner. Having said this, however, this quite common view of parents often, in itself, reflects a 'stuck' kind of perspective which can often be overcome by a change in attitude.

It is true that not all parents have good skills in relating, and not all parents have wisdom to offer about finding a mate. Fortunately, there are others who can help. If you know adults who appear to have a good marriage, ask them questions. None of them may have a final word, but you are almost sure to learn much that can be helpful. Since marriage is a social institution, it makes sense that relating to others openly is a good way in.

If you are a loner, get over your reservations about relating to people if you are contemplating marriage, because marriage is all about relating. If you think you cannot talk to others whom you deem trustworthy, then you need to work on yourself until you can do this. It is, of course, possible to find a partner without getting over all your hang-ups about people, but this 'closed' approach to the world will put way too much of a burden on your partner. Learn to open your world before looking for a partner. Learn to trust others.

Having discussed the importance of being able to turn to others while on the path of search, I want to write a few words about why I have emphasized the usefulness of turning to older people. It is important to have friends who are of your own age group, but it is a mistake to make these the only ones you confide in unless you happen to be an older single and your friends have a solidly good marriage. The relationship 'scene' may be made up of primarily young people, but I will emphasize again that marriage is of another order of relationship than having boyfriends or girlfriends, having sexual relationships, or even living together and having children together. Peer friendships, while important, are not usually a very good source of wisdom when it comes to issues and questions about marriage. We will see later how much our relationship with our parents will inevitably influence our marital relationships. Marriage is not just a social institution, it is ultimately the core of a cross-generational matrix of relationships. If, before marriage, we have forged healthy, open relationships with people of different generations, this augers well for our future marriage.

There is a trend among youth not to pay heed to what adults say about things, to close them off and turn to our peer group for support and perhaps advice. Adults are not gods, but when it comes to marriage, a long view of things is valuable. We can learn from the mistakes made by adults and, especially, we can learn from those whose marriages have withstood tests and are thriving. Having open relationships with people of different generations is a sign of maturity and readiness to marry; its lack, a sign that something is missing.

Prayer and meditation

We started this chapter by discussing our individual capacity for delusion and our tendency to persist in what we want, disregarding our higher good. Amongst peers, there is a collective tendency to delusion and wilfulness, and this is another reason why I have underlined the importance of looking to different generations to help gain perspective on questions about marriage. But even when we are open and willing to turn to others for help, there is something which is very individual and personal in finding a marriage partner. The choices we ultimately make are always going to be ours. Even if we let someone else decide for us what course to take, it is our choice to do that, and therefore, our responsibility. We can weigh all the best advice of books and others, but the ultimate weighing and choosing is done by us alone, with all of our capacity for delusion and, these days, coupled with a huge collective rate of failures in marriage. If we are honest with ourselves, given the gravity of the stakes, the prospect of finding someone to share our lives with is a frightening one.

• • • • • • • • • •

When I was a kid, I used to pray every night for a new bicycle.
Then I realized that the Lord doesn't work that way,
so I just stole one and asked Him to forgive me.

Emo Philips

• • • • • • • • • •

There is help for us in this existential dilemma. Besides being a social institution, marriage is also a spiritual one. It is in the realm of the spirit that things come together, that stuck situations are transformed, that fear is transmuted into confidence. The spiritual facets and challenges of marriage call for us to be spiritually developed and prepared, and for this the practice of prayer and meditation is crucial.

• • • • • • • • • •

To pray is to pay attention to something or someone
other than oneself.
Whenever a man so concentrates his attention
– on a landscape, a poem, a geometrical problem, an idol,
or the Living God –
that he completely forgets his own ego and desires,
he is praying.

W. H. Auden

• • • • • • • • • •

Prayer is not simply asking God for what you want. Prayer is, first of all, giving utterance to the most plain and bare-faced truths of our human reality: that without spiritual assistance we have neither the knowledge nor the power to attain the goal for which we were created. The only really worthy desire is to seek that which our Creator wants for us. Perhaps what we want is what God wants for us, but the attitude of prayer is one of humility, of going inside, then expressing what we believe is best for us, then testing it – in word – to see if it resonates with that highest truth: that only God really knows what is best and the only real satisfaction is contentment with what this is. Prayer is the opportunity we create to bring our egos into line with our soul's yearning, a kind of tuning up without which our actions are bound to grate against our higher aspirations. Of course, even after tuning up we can still go out of tune, but without having tuned up at all we will not likely even recognize the state of tunefulness.

Psychologically speaking, health is in part the ability to face reality as it is with full and unblocked energy. Some people think pessimism is a way of seeing things as they really are, but pessimism is really just selectively seeing and anticipating failure. Prayer is a positive recognition of higher reality and an expression

· · · · · · · · · ·

. . . the sign of the intellect is contemplation and the sign of contemplation is silence,
because it is impossible for a man to do two things at one time
– he cannot both speak and meditate.
It is an axiomatic fact that while you meditate you are speaking with your own spirit.
In that state of mind you put certain questions to your spirit and the spirit answers;
the light breaks forth and the reality is revealed.
'Abdu'l-Bahá

· · · · · · · · · ·

of faith in this higher reality. The higher reality is spiritual; it may not as yet be realized, but it is no less real in its possibility. A failure to acknowledge or pursue this innate spiritual reality cuts us off from this source of truth and can make of our best efforts an exercise in futility.

Meditation is time given to quiet reflection. There are many ways to meditate but, as revealed in the above quotation, meditation requires us to be silent. In order to make our minds quiet, we may need some preparation and exercise, but the process of meditation is ultimately a 'going inside'. Reading from sacred writings and great thinkers can feed our meditation and provide a source of inspiration. Reflecting on these and meditating on how our lives and actions compare with the counsels of God or inspired thinkers is good food for thought. This is a very private but essential practice for anyone who is conscious that we are spiritual beings on a spiritual path. Furthermore, finding – and maintaining – our spiritual ground is essential to the process of finding and developing a relationship with a potential marriage partner.

Action

• • • • • • • • • •

Prayer and meditation
are very important factors in deepening
the spiritual life of the individual,
but with them must go also action and example,
as these are the tangible results of the former.
Both are essential.

On behalf of Shoghi Effendi

• • • • • • • • • •

The next step is action itself, meaning that we cannot lock ourselves up in our homes and wait until a partner knocks at our door. But where we go is an important factor in determining whom we are likely to encounter and how we may meet or get to know someone. There are night clubs and discos where many young singles can be found, but for several reasons I rule these out as good venues for finding a partner. First of all, these are entertainment venues. While they may be fitting for having a good time, if we are looking for someone who shares our significant interests and goals, the venues developed for having fun do not work very well. True, some who are there may share some of your significant interests, but how do you find that out? These places are usually noisy, conversations difficult, and the only way to really get to know someone better is to get out. But even if you find someone you are interested in a place like this and you make the move to be with him or her somewhere else so that you can better learn about each other, then you have already made a move which precludes certain important learning opportunities. What you miss in taking these steps will be covered more thoroughly in Chapter 6 where it is stressed that observing the other from afar, **before motions towards courtship are made**, is an important stage in getting to know what he or she is really like. Observing people in the atmosphere of a disco yields very little useful knowledge.

The kind of venue that probably best serves the interests of finding a potential partner are the places you go to serve your higher interests and your spirituality. Thus, developing an attitude of service, of being part of something beyond you, whether you are religious or not, not only enhances your spiritual development, but will lead you to places that will bring you into contact with others in a more conscious, meaningful way. Environmental projects, special interest groups, charities and various volunteer groups can all provide good occasions for meeting potential mates. Informal gatherings of friends and acquaintances can also be good – I hesitate to say parties, because the atmosphere of these are most often 'driven' by alcohol or high decibel music, neither of which is conducive to the kind of consciousness I have been talking about. Being willing to try new things, take classes, join clubs, choruses, drama groups, dance groups – all these serve to bring you into contact with others who are more likely to share a lot in common with you and who are more likely to look at relationships maturely.

In this regard, being a member of a religious community can be a great advantage. Getting involved with your place of worship or visiting other religious gatherings can be enriching, and both can provide good opportunities to get to know others in a mindful way. Bahá'ís have a great variety of such possibilities because the orientation of a healthy Bahá'í community is to reach out, to travel, to visit, to serve the wider community and the Bahá'í community itself. These are all wonderful opportunities to widen one's social horizons and to bring one into contact with others who have an orientation to serve and to develop themselves spiritually. Even though most Bahá'í communities are still quite small and possibilities within them may seem limited, travelling to serve, to do a year of service, to go to summer schools in different localities, to get involved in the process of growth now taking place in Bahá'í communities, meeting with people of other religions – these all provide opportunities to enrich one's soul and it is precisely these kinds of activities that will bring singles into contact with others who have a similar orientation. There are three influences upon our mind set which are relevant here.

Unconscious mindsets

Jesus said 'seek, and ye shall find'. When we are searching for something, it is important to be aware of our spiritual nature and to develop a spiritual attitude. What this is differs greatly from our usual, day-to-day mindset. Psychologically speaking, our day-to-day mindset is most often a replay of thoughts and attitudes from our past, or images fed to us daily in the media. Both of these primary sources play repeatedly in our minds, guiding our actions, usually with us being unaware of what is happening. We all need to wake up to these influences and combat them if we are to gain control of our destiny, and this relates very directly to finding a mate.

The influence of childhood experience on mindset

The deepest source of the counterproductive attitudes which tend to guide our actions and thoughts comes from difficult or traumatic – perhaps even forgotten – past experiences and family patterns. If we lack confidence and self-esteem, the reason can usually be found in our past experience. Even if we do not remember the experiences themselves, they live on through the repeated messages we send ourselves countless times throughout the day. For example, let us say you had difficulties in school. Certain concepts may not have been presented correctly to you or they may have been presented prematurely, and you could not get a handle on them. Especially if teachers or parents were impatient with you in this process, you might very well have internalized a message like 'I am stupid. I can't do anything right.' The essence of your early experience will be carried forward through repeated self-talk like this whenever you face a challenge. Studies have shown that when people are feeling low or defeated, messages like this go through their head approximately 600 times a day! This, of course, is a recipe for defeat, but most of us never take the time to really take a look at what these thoughts are, or how illogical they are, or how we can replace them with truer, more productive messages.

In the process of socialization, many girls are not given positive reinforcement for being assertive or thinking clearly, and often internalize a message that they are not valued for these qualities, but only for being pretty or doing what men like. Many boys internalize the message that they have to be aggressive, strong and have sexual experience if they are to be judged a 'man'. These internalized messages pull many males and females into negative relationship patterns and need to be consciously countered.

The influence of the media on mindset

The influence of the media is a whole study in itself, but let me just take a little time to bring to light some of its main themes which relate to finding a mate. One oft-repeated message found in various media these days is that you are nothing without sex appeal. This message is not usually conveyed directly in words, but in images. Even if words are used, they are used to paint an image which often conveys this message. Images are registered largely by the right side of our brain and are not logically scrutinized – logic is a function, primarily, of the left side of the brain. Unless we take the time to analyse what the messages fed to us in image form are, they will swim in our brains, influencing our actions and choices in many ways. The message that we are nothing without sex appeal is both negative and counterproductive unless all you really want out of life is mindless fun. In fact, the unspoken ubiquitous message of modern media is that mindless fun is really what life is about! As an image, this is very attractive and enticing; as a basis for a meaningful existence, it is empty and harmful.

Another underlying media message of today is that whatever we want we should have, and have it right now. Buying into this attitude will ultimately sell us short. Discipline and steadfastness are needed in order to achieve worthy results in our life. Instant gratification is just another aspect of the enticing media view that life is about mindless fun and it is another attitude which serves to undermine our essentially spiritual nature and the sacred nature of finding a life partner. We need to be awake and thoughtful – even wary – while on the path of search. We need, therefore, to counter these subliminal messages and consciously develop a more spiritual orientation.

Social myths and mindset

There are a number of widely circulated – and usually seldom questioned – social views or attitudes that also need to be identified, then scrutinized. These may have to do with prejudices. Many prejudices are quite unconscious but affect a broad spectrum of people. Most of us do not like to think we have racist attitudes, but our societies are replete with them and, unless we dig deeply, we will never uncover them. If you have counted out the possibility of courting someone of another race – **any other race** – then you can be quite sure that you have internalized certain prejudices about certain racial groups, and these need to be brought to light and countered. We are all humans living together in a world that has contracted into a global village. There is no room for the kind of exclusive attitudes which most of our forbears had. There are other prejudices like this pertaining to class, wealth, dress, occupation, handicaps – all of these need to be closely examined.

Building a conscious mindset

What can we do about these persistent messages which we internalize from our early experience, or from the constant exposure to various media, or broadly socially reinforced opinions, or unconscious attitudes – messages which could undermine our quest to have a successful marriage? First we must learn to counter the negative or counter-productive self-talk; second, we must develop a mindset with a spiritual base. Let me tackle these two in order.

Taking control of our mindset

There are three steps to be taken if we want to overcome the negative influence of our own self-talk. Let us take the above example of the person who, because of negative experiences in school, has come to repeat, internally, 'I am stupid. I can't do anything right.' The first step would be to objectify this thought that is daily swimming in our consciousness. To do this, we need to write the thought down. These thoughts can be best identified when we are not feeling good, because that is when they repeat themselves the most. Unfortunately, when we don't feel good, we don't usually feel like doing anything constructive, so the thoughts tend to take over. Don't let them just go on and on; the simple, but necessary, step to take is to write the thoughts down.

Once the thought has been exposed and is on paper, you have already taken some of the power out of it. But there is more to do. Look at the statement rationally. You may think you have already done this by coming to the conclusion that this is simply the truth, but this statement is never true in any person's case. The seeming truth of this kind of statement is circular and self-fulfilling. Saying 'I can't do anything right' will lead you to make mistakes, and many of the mistakes you have made in the past were simply the result of repeating this irrational mantra. Take a more adult look at the statement. If a friend of yours said this about himself, would you tell him 'Yeah, you're right, you *are* stupid!'? No, you wouldn't. So start by being a friend to yourself. Give yourself the benefit of the doubt for a moment and look at the truth value of this statement more rationally. Parents, teachers, schools – people and their institutions all make mistakes, but an ideal educator or educational system will be careful to present material in a digestible form, suited to the individual learner. Every individual can learn in this way. If we have failed in our **early** upbringing, the failure is not ours but the system's. Further, none of us fail at everything. We have all learned a difficult language – our mother tongue - and we all do some things well. Why should we trivialize these accomplishments or reduce their significance by comparing ourselves with others who do better? Look again at the statement 'I can't do anything right,' and write beside it in bold letters: **'Wrong!'** Then identify how it is wrong, again, in writing. For example, 'This statement is untrue, first of all because it ignores my past accomplishments; secondly, because it prophesies future actions which cannot be known or anticipated.'

The next step is to correct the offending, patently irrational statement. It might go something like this: 'I have struggled with learning many things but I have had success with others. I am an able person, ready to move ahead in life and learn new, even difficult things if they are presented in an appropriate way.' This, now, is a rational, healthy assessment of who you are and what you can do. Now let this new formulation feed your actions and decisions. You may take this further by distilling its essence and putting it in the front of your mind at important and repeated intervals. For example, take the statement 'I am an able person, ready to move forward in life'. Write it down, keep it in your mind's eye, remind yourself of it regularly, and let it become your mantra. Remember, it is competing with up to 600 times a day for the other, illogical, undermining statement that you started with.

Now that we have followed through one example of a mental message that is a distortion of the truth and learned how to transform it into a statement which is both more sound rationally and emotionally more empowering, let us look at some other typical examples of self-talk which we internalize from our childhood or from the media and see how they might be similarly trans-formed. Some of these will be specifically for men; others for women.

· · · · · · · · · ·

Fear is nothing but faith in reverse gear.
The foundation on which both faith and fear rest is belief in
something.

Napoleon Hill

· · · · · · · · · ·

1. Self-talk:
   I really screwed that up. I might as well give up.
   Rational transformation:
   I could have done that better. I'll see what I can do to make things better.

2. Self-talk (for women):
   Men are only after me for my body.
   Rational transformation:
   I am a woman with a mind of my own and many worthy qualities. Men can also be interested in the qualities of mind and heart, I can pass by those who are not.

3. Self-talk:

I will never be able to do this. ('This' could be almost anything.)

Rational transformation:

This is going to be a challenge, but what is life without challenges? I am going to give it my best.

• • • • • • • • • •

When you've exhausted all possibilities, remember this:
You haven't.

Robert H. Schuller

• • • • • • • • • •

4. Self-talk:

I have done every thing I could. (Usually when we tell ourselves this we have been just spinning our wheels, repeating the same kind of mistake over and over again.)

Rational transformation:

There is probably something that will work. I may have to look at this from a different perspective if I am going to be successful.

5. Self-talk:

It's not going to work.

Rational transformation:

If it is God's will I can make this work.

6. Self-talk:

I will never find a partner. (Now you are playing God, predicting your future!)

Rational transformation:

I am open to finding a partner. There might be much that I have to do to prepare myself and I need to learn patience.

7. Self-talk:

No man/woman will find me interesting.

Rational transformation:

I have many qualities that the right person will find attractive and I am working on improving myself every day.

8. Self-talk

All men/women are the same.

Rational transformation:

Every man/woman is unique and many do not fit the usual pattern, some that do just need a 'wake-up' call.

9. Self-talk (for men):

Women don't like gentle, sensitive men.

Rational transformation:

Many women are sick of men who are loud and aggressive. If I put myself forward, I am sure to find a suitable woman who is interested in my quieter nature.

10. Self-talk:

I can't make changes, what will my friends think?

Rational transformation:

Some people are threatened by change, but I am open to it. I can make new friends if I need to.

11. Self-talk (for women):

Men are after sex. If I don't give in they will find someone else.

Rational transformation:

Many men go for sex because they do not know any better. If I demand respect, I will find men who show respect, the others I can do without.

12. Self-talk (for men):

If I don't have a sexual relationship with my girl friend, my friends will think I am strange or impotent.

Rational transformation:

I respect my partner and can feel proud of my own values. I can express myself with confidence about this and if others think I'm strange, that's their problem.

13. Self-talk:

I can't trust anyone.

Rational transformation:

I can learn to trust, but I need to keep my eyes open.

14. Self-talk:

I am going to get hurt again if I get into this.

Rational transformation:

If I have given myself time, and worked through the grieving process from my last relationship, I can learn from the lessons of my past mistakes and move forward.

15. Self-talk (for women):

I shouldn't speak my mind because men won't find me attractive.

Rational transformation:

I have a good mind and can feel good in expressing myself freely and respectfully. Men who are threatened by this strength need to learn to grow up.

The above is just a sampling of some of the self-talk and internalized messages that keep us stuck or invite failure, and the suggested transformations are not the only possibilities. You can discover your own internalized messages and come up with your own transformations. Be creative but clear. As you open to this process, you will discover more of these negative messages which circle in your head or in the media or in your family or social circles. Change your thinking and you can change your experience.

A spiritual mindset

• • • • • • • • • •

As you have faith, so shall your powers and blessings be.

'Abdu'l-Bahá

• • • • • • • • • •

Although the previous section was primarily a psychological use of cognitive behavioural techniques to change counterproductive messages we may have internalized, using them has already helped us to establish some spiritual ground. Many of the rational transformations above contain an element of faith – for example: I can learn to trust; I'll do better next time. Faith is something we can nurture and pray for at all times and is both a psychological and spiritual ingredient necessary for a fulfilling life.

But let us now look more earnestly at what it means to have a spiritual attitude when searching. Many people just move into relationships with fuzzy, unexamined romantic and/or sexual images swirling around their heads, and the confusing and hurtful results of this can be anticipated from the outset. A spiritual mindset is a responsible one – one where we will exercise the qualities of our soul and keep our relationship with our Creator at the forefront. Patience, love, hope, joy, detachment, and service – these are among the spiritual qualities we can call forth while on the path of search.

Patience

• • • • • • • • • •

The steed of this Valley [of Search] is patience;
without patience the wayfarer on this journey will reach
nowhere and attain no goal.
Nor should he ever be downhearted . . .

Bahá'u'lláh

• • • • • • • • • •

Among the qualities we need to develop while on the path of search are equanimity and patience. These are spiritual qualities without which we fall into anxiety and discouragement. Finding a mate will be one of the most momentous turning points in our life. We cannot expect it to happen overnight or in our own imagining of what an appropriate amount of time might be. If it seems to take a long time, it may be that we have not been open to certain new areas of our own personal development, one of which may simply be the need to develop patience. Patience includes elements of enthusiasm, awareness and alertness. Patience is an active state as opposed to a feeling of passive helplessness or apathy. Discouragement should not enter into our vocabulary, for we do not know what lessons we may need to learn in this process. All learning processes involve making mistakes. This is not negative: every mistake we make, when reflected upon, adds to our knowledge.

Love

. . . .

And those souls whose inner being is lit by the love of God
are even as spreading rays of light,
and they will shine out like stars of holiness in a pure
and crystalline sky.

'Abdu'l-Bahá

. . . .

The writings of the world's religions are replete with the subject of divine love. Loving our creative Source eliminates anxiety and fills us with spirit. As implied in the above quotation, loving God makes us more attractive to souls, it makes us 'shine'. This is both an inner gift and an outwardly visible quality that will help us attract a worthy partner.

Hope

· · · · · · · · · ·

Man is under all conditions immersed in a sea of God's blessings.
Therefore, be thou not hopeless under any circumstances,
but rather firm in thy hope.

'Abdu'l-Bahá

· · · · · · · · · ·

As suggested in the above quotation, being without hope is a sign of being disconnected from blessings which are actually flooding down upon us at all times. Giving up hope is a recipe for depression, and depression is dysfunctional and never brings us toward our heart's desire. Hope keeps our mind alert to new possibilities and creative solutions. Hope, like love, is also a point of attraction, while depression does just the opposite.

Joy

· · · · · · · · · ·

Let us neither make known our sufferings nor complain of our
wrongs.
Rather let us become oblivious of our own selves,
And drinking down the wine of heavenly grave,
Let us cry out our joy . . .

'Abdu'l-Bahá

· · · · · · · · · ·

Joy is something that blossoms forth from our inmost being when we are in touch with our spiritual Source. Lack of joy is a sign that we are immersed in our own selves. Joy is not a Pollyannish surface sweetness. Rather, joy comes from spiritual depth. In a TV interview, the Dalai Lama drew a comparison with the ocean: on the surface we may be beset with – and affected by – trials and sorrows, just as the ocean produces waves in storms and wind; but beneath the surface the depths are calm, serene and undisturbed. This is, by analogy, the deep source of joy which is born of spirit.

Detachment

• • • • • • • • • •

Ask not of Me that which We desire not for thee,
then be content with what We have ordained for thy sake,
for this is that which profiteth thee,
if therewith thou dost content thyself.

Bahá'u'lláh

• • • • • • • • • •

Detachment is crucial to the process of seeking. If we can detach ourselves from our own expectations, we can see more clearly; if we can detach ourselves from a certain end product, we can find equanimity and spiritual contentment in the process. Remember, we are constantly drawn to our ego's desires but these are a chimera. With detachment we are enabled to let go of these distractions and keep ourselves on a path that leads us to our goal.

Service

• • • • • • • • • •

Man's merit lieth in service and virtue . . .

Bahá'u'lláh

• • • • • • • • • •

Part of readying and developing ourselves includes an orientation of service in whatever we are doing. This is another spiritual requirement, not just of searching, but of life. Living to promote the betterment of others and of humanity as a whole is part and parcel of the purpose of life. The purpose of finding a partner is not to be free of loneliness or to enjoy the thrills of falling in love, rather, it is to find someone who will be an intimate partner in our path of service and one with whom we can have children who will also be reared in an attitude of serving the good of humanity. A worthy goal of living and building a life together is to contribute to the betterment of the world. If service is our orientation, we are actually less prone to the anxieties of waiting and wondering and, ultimately, we are much more likely to be brought into meaningful contact with someone we share that orientation with and who is more likely to make a good wife or good husband.

✷✷✷   ✷✷✷   ✷✷✷

The primary message of this chapter is that we are on a quest, one that is – if we see it correctly – a spiritual one. Unfortunately, much of what is 'out there' in the world, in our present society, is likely to pull us away from this spiritual essence and draw us towards a materialistic or physically based way of seeing things, a way that will lead inevitably to delusion or worry. We need always to come back to this spiritual ground and remind ourselves of the sacredness of the path we are walking. Developing a spiritual mindset will give us the means of identifying and rooting out materialistic or egoistic attitudes and will help keep us on a healthy path; this, in turn, will attract confirmations from our spiritual source. But let us now continue along the path and look more closely at the nature of attraction, for choices will need to be made and we will need to have our eyes open

4

Attraction

In most parts of the modern world we have come to consider it our right to select our own mate. But we did not always have this 'right', and in some parts of the world marriages are still contracted by parents of the couple or other elders. Before we turn up our noses at this apparently archaic practice, it should be noted that divorce rates are actually usually lower when the individual does not choose his or her own partner. This should give us some pause for reflection: 'Why does our more modern approach have such a poor track record?'

Human freedom

The modern Western world has shifted towards an orientation of greater freedom. It seems quite apparent that this is a step from which we are not likely to retreat. Most of the rest of the world is moving in this direction; where it isn't, a hunger for more freedom can be perceived. Thus, even though divorce rates have risen – at least partly – because of greater individual freedom, even the most conservative elements of our societies are not suggesting that we should sacrifice this freedom in the hope of retrieving the kind of stability families had in the past.

The societies where elders choose mates for their youth tend to have family structures that are rigid and much less democratic. Grandparents and other relatives are not involved in the working family, but often dominate. This interference often creates extreme problems for the nuclear members of the family, especially for those in the weakest positions. In the past there may have been a kind of comfort and security in this extended family system, the pressure of responsibility less onerous for the parents, but the increase of individual empowerment in the nuclear family system seems to be what is winning the day. The consequence of this shift is that couples are left on their own shouldering financial concerns and the ever-growing complexity of childrearing and children's education. We want our freedom but for the most part we have not yet learned to handle the responsibility in a healthy manner. Stuck in an adolescent phase, we still tend to want freedom without fully appreciating the responsibility it entails. We also tend to want to doggedly go it alone, refusing the perspective of elders which could help us. Further, too much insistence on individuality can leave us feeling isolated and rob us of the potential which lies in finding healthy ways of involving our extended family. In sum, a healthy balance between unbridled individualism and rigid social control has not yet been found.

· · · · · · · · · ·

Love is blind but marriage is an eye opener
Anonymous

· · · · · · · · · ·

Like many of the individual freedoms we have won or adopted, choosing a marriage partner is a freedom with a double-edged sword. If the ultimate choice is going to be ours, we need to be prepared to live with it and make it work. Like brash young adolescents, we have tended to set out with a sense of abandon: 'It's my choice; I'll do what I want. Stay out of my way.' But why not pause to reflect upon the gravity such choice entails? The conscious soul, awake to the many ways in which our passions and desires can lead us astray and hamper our objectivity, will be happy to recognize that it also has the freedom to consult with others about this crucial question, and will be happy to seek out the help of wiser, older and more experienced minds who will take the time to help us on our path.

Who do we look for?

• • • • • • • • • •

Why the hell should I get a wife
when the man next door's got one?

'Furry' Lewis

• • • • • • • • • •

Once we are clear that the ultimate responsibility for mate selection falls upon our own shoulders and we find ourselves 'out there' in the field of singles (we are assuming, here, that no explanation is needed regarding the fact that those who are already married are 'out of bounds'), one of the first issues to come to terms with is attraction. Who are we attracted to? Who finds us attractive? What brings a man and a woman together when outside forces, such as the tradition of parents selecting a mate for their children, are no longer there? Is there just one 'right' person out there for me and is it my task to find that one? Is there such a thing as 'love at first sight'?

Attraction to someone of the opposite sex occurs at various levels and, not surprisingly, much of what we feel as attraction has unconscious sources. Consciously, we develop ideals about what kind of person would be good for us and what they should look like, etc. We also develop ideas about what kind of person to avoid. How much we develop these conscious ideas varies greatly from person to person. Sometimes we have very strong ideas about what kind of person we would like as a partner but have not actually given much careful thought to it. Our ideas are influenced by popular notions, media, peers and so forth.

As I have already stated, the attraction that most of us have to the opposite sex is partly biological, and partly because of their difference and the mystery and curiosity that goes along with this difference. But the fears and prejudices that go along with encountering foreign worlds and the tendency of our ego boundaries to resist encounters with 'the other' can often offset our attractions. Thus, there are factors that that lead us to be interested and attracted and other factors that incline us to keep distant and be wary.

A very powerful source of attraction is the sexual or hormonal one. In its pure form, it is not selective at all. For this most primitive source of attraction to exert its full force, some physical proximity is required. Usually our ego boundaries and social training act as an impediment to this happening. The means of breaking through this barrier also tend to be quite primitive: they include alcohol, drugs, erotic media and other means of creating a sexually charged atmosphere. In other words, for this most simple form of attraction to exert its influence we have to circumvent our usual sense of self-respect and social awareness. Even for those who purposely engage in this most gross kind of sexual attraction, it is not usually for the purpose of selecting a mate. When the partners wake up out of their stupor they are likely to find that their sexual partner is entirely unsuitable as a life partner. When, and if, they really wake up, they will also realize that they themselves are not really suitable as a life partner yet.

Biology

• • • • • • • • • •

An archaeologist is the best husband any woman can have;
the older she gets, the more interested he is in her.

Agatha Christie

• • • • • • • • • •

Beyond the pure power of sexual attraction, there are theories that have been put forward to explain what it is that draws two people together for the purpose of mating. I will explore here those that have been reviewed by Harville Hendrix in *Getting the Love You Want*. The most basic of these is derived from biology and Darwin's evolutionary view of the survival of the fittest. In this view, we have a biological instinct to select a mate who will help our species to survive. Men, accordingly, are drawn to women who are young, look healthy, and are able to bear children. Thus, for men, youth – and signs of youth – are important. Bone structure, clear skin, full lips, eyes that are 'awake' and large, these signs of classical beauty have, according to biologists, an instinctual appeal to men which makes it more likely that their mate will be able to bear them lots of healthy children and serve, ultimately, to enhance the preservation of their species. Some interesting studies have shown that men are attracted by the body odour of some women and not of others and that the genes of those women whose scent they are attracted to combine well with their own genes in such a way that if they were to have children it is less likely that their children would suffer from genetic diseases or disorders.

For women, the biological criteria of attraction are somewhat different. Women will look for men who have the capacity to dominate others, to take charge, to show the ability and confidence to be in control. This is because the woman is, at this primitive level, looking for a man who has the capacity to protect her while she bears and nurtures children. According to this view, it is not as important to women that men be young or even handsome. Women, young or old, are more likely to be attracted to men who have achieved some kind of success in the world or appear to be in charge of their own destiny. Interestingly, studies have shown that during the few days of their menstrual cycle when women are ovulating, they are more attracted to men whose faces appear more masculine, whereas throughout the rest of their cycle they may tend to be more interested in softer, more feminine characteristics in a man's face.

Clearly, this biological model of sexual attraction does not take into account the many finer, higher, and more subtle aspects of human functioning. Nevertheless, we ignore these biological insights at our peril. Precisely because the human creature is much more complex than a purely biological being, we need to become aware of primitive and unconscious urges because they may easily drive us towards selecting a totally unsuitable mate at totally unsuitable times. These 'basic instincts' drive the fashion and cosmetics industries and have a huge influence on much that we see in the various media. Many middle-aged men give up on their marriages and family life to fall for a young woman who in turn is attracted to him despite his age and marital status, because of his social position, confidence and stature. Young women can fall for 'macho' men because they appear strong and confident – but find, once married, that their males' egos are frail, that they seem incapable of tenderness and lack responsibility. Thus, while we are searching out more encompassing theories of romantic attraction, let us not keep our eyes closed to the role of more primitive urges, not least so that we will be less likely to fall into their trap.

Exchange theory

Social psychologists have proposed an 'exchange' theory of mate selection. This theory recognizes the capacity we have to select a mate on a variety of levels at the same time. This, it is proposed, is usually done almost instantaneously whenever we meet someone and are in the mode of looking for a partner. According to this theory, what we are looking for is someone who 'matches' us, someone who is basically on the same level whether it is with respect to their looks, financial status, intelligence, morality or other facets of their personality.

Exchange theory helps us to understand that humans are usually more selective than purely biological or evolutionary factors would predict. The process of sizing up the other, though fast, is not necessarily entirely out of our consciousness.

According to this view, our initial impressions of another can be quite comprehensive and accurate. What is unconscious in the process is that we are looking for someone who is not much better than us, according to the various factors of selection. The same applies to financial status, social status, intelligence, creativity and so on. We may not like to admit it to ourselves, but we do not usually want to be outclassed by our partner in any of these areas. In fact, some studies have shown that if one or the other in a marriage feels less than their partner, the resulting insecurity does not auger well for the relationship. This theory shows that there are usually a number of factors that can enter into the process of mate selection and that the qualities a person has can be very important to us.

The persona

Another aspect of mate selection has been suggested by Jung. This appears to be somewhat in opposition to exchange theory. We have already discussed Jung's belief that we each have a persona, or mask, that we present to the outside world. This mask is one of the ways our ego protects itself. It is part of the myth that we carry about ourselves and what we want others to see in us. When it comes to mate selection, what this aspect of our self attempts to do is enhance itself, that is, to prop up our self-image. According to this dynamic, how our mate appears to others and the degree to which he or she bolsters our own persona is very important to us and has a significant influence on our choice.

The need for a new theory

All these theories contain truth, but do they really satisfy us or explain our attractions adequately? Falling in love is a powerful experience which raises our sense of aliveness to peak levels, tears down our usual defences, and wreaks havoc with our preconceptions. The experience of falling in love even breaks through our ego boundaries, those very carefully-built-up means of survival that we erected in our early childhood when faced with the perceived terrors of abandonment when we first woke up to our dependence and vulnerability. When we fall in love, lost hope is restored, and we feel perfectly cared for, ready to conquer the world. None of the foregoing theories of attraction would predict such an all-encompassing, super-intensive experience and ecstasy to which the human creature can fall prey when love strikes.

Another aspect of human relationships which the theories described above fail to account for is the other side of romantic bliss: the experience of breaking up. The pain and loss felt by couples who break up, the deep pit of the bereavement into which they fall, would not be expected as a by-product of the theories we have described. Somehow, when people fall in love and get involved with each other, incredibly deep attachments are formed. None of the above forces of attraction explain the deeper levels of human contact and the relationship of this to the kind of person who attracts us in the first place. Romantic attraction is powerful and unrequited attraction deeply disappointing. The theories do not account for the depth of despair felt by those whose romantic hopes are dashed.

· · · · · · · · · ·

A divorce is like an amputation; you survive,
but there's less of you.

Margaret Atwood

· · · · · · · · · ·

Further to this, we humans tend to be much more selective than any of the above theories can account for. Most of us have contact with hundreds, even thousands, of potential partners before we find one with whom there is a strong mutual attraction. In addition, Harville Hendrix has noted, those who break up with their partner tend to be attracted to someone who resembles the one (or ones) they have broken up with. This pattern of seeking out a partner with strikingly similar characteristics is not done consciously. Many people who have been through a series of relationships begin to doubt themselves – or even to doubt the existence of good potential marriage partners – because they experience this kind of pattern over and over again. None of us would consciously want to repeat the suffering that we go through in a relationship that doesn't work, yet the fact is, most of us tend to do just that. What is it that seems to propel us towards certain types of individual and not others? Why do some have such potential to ignite flames of passion and, on the other side, pull us into deep depression when it doesn't work out?

· · · · · · · · · ·

I am still going on bad dates,
when by now I should be in a bad marriage.

Laura Kightlinger

· · · · · · · · · ·

Imago

To explain these factors of mate selection, Hendrix says that we have to look to our deep unconscious mechanisms for an answer. Although we do not have conscious memory of most of our most formative years, our brain has continued to store, in some form, the essence of these experiences. A significant aspect of what is stored in our brains is a painful emotional record of growing up. In Chapter 1 we touched upon the fact that socialization and growing up necessarily entails pain, even in healthy well-functioning families. Of course, our parents, siblings and others within our family circle are most closely associated with both the pains and joys of growing up. These most crucial memories and associations are stored in the limbic system, part of the 'old' or more primitive part of our brain. The old brain is that part which determines our more automatic behaviour, and within it the limbic system generates vivid emotions. According to Hendrix, embedded in our old brain is a kind of picture which represents the painfully familiar traits of our primary caregivers. This he calls our Imago.

In this theory, our encounters with potential partners are unconsciously measured against our Imago. When the fit is good, the sense of familiarity generates interest and excitement. In this view, the old brain influences our choice of a mate in such a way that we tend to unconsciously recreate the environment of our childhood. Guided by our Imago, we tend to select a mate with both the positive and negative qualities of those most intimately involved in our upbringing. Even when the resulting relationship fails, we usually look for the same kind of fit in our next partner.

Although this may sound quite negative, Hendrix quite rightly takes the view that we are not doomed to repeat the mistakes and patterns of our forebears. Rather, we present ourselves with familiar facets of our childhood in our mate selection so that we can heal the wounds from that period and recover our wholeness. I call this the trick of God. None of us consciously wants to repeat the painfully raw experiences from our childhood, so God has provided us with a mechanism whereby we become seduced by the beauty of those who will lead us to do just that. This becomes our unparalleled opportunity for growth, if we can see it as such.

I would like to add here that although I believe Hendrix is right about our unconscious tendency, the question of attraction is still not decisively answered. To some degree, our unconscious processes are bound to win out in the end, but there are conscious processes that can lead us to a much happier context for working out the unmet needs of our childhood. For example, being conscious that finding a partner will necessarily lead us into the dark abyss of our childhood experience, we would do well to find a partner who is equally awake to this reality, willing to make the journey, and open to learning healthy processes of working through these primal issues without running away. Beyond this, we can undertake to discover and become more conscious of our Imago, and work towards healing the wounds from our childhood to some degree. How much we are able to do this will make us more whole and will, therefore, attract us toward more healthy partners. I would hasten to add, however, that there is nothing quite as potent as marriage itself for providing the opportunity for healing, and I do not believe we should put off indefinitely taking this more ultimate step in the interest of 'preparing ourselves'. Those with clear factors of dysfunction in their families of origin – drug abuse, alcoholism, physical and sexual abuse, however – would do well to work through these issues with a therapist before looking seriously for a mate.

With open eyes

• • • • • • • • • •

We have to realize that we are as deeply afraid to live and love as we are to die.

R. D. Laing

• • • • • • • • • •

Most of us enter into thoughts of marriage out of a feeling of loneliness, a yearning for romance, an escape from our parents, or other essentially self-serving reasons. Marriage is not at its heart any of these things. It does serve the self, but in a much more profound way. In marriage, we are bound to run into difficulties that will challenge us to the quick. Our initial gut-level reaction to these kinds of deep challenges is to reject them, to say in one manner or another, 'I want out.' We experience these challenges as an echo of our primal pain in growing up and we want to strike out or escape. In other words, we tend to experience the trials of marriage as victims and ask ourselves, 'Why me?' or, if we are able to hear the primal echoes we will ask, rather, 'This, again?'

Lao Tse has written: 'Because the superior man seeks out difficulties, he experiences none.' From this we can understand that the wise or superior person will not feel the kind of pain that life and marriage inevitably bring in the same way that a 'victim' does, because he or she purposely sets out to confront the difficulties that such significant steps in living entail. A person can then recognize and remember his or her own choice in the matter and take responsibility for it. It is only insofar as we are able to do this in marriage that we can taste the sweetest fruits of this profound union.

This is primarily where consciousness comes in. Our eyes are open to the challenges ahead of us and, with a maximum degree of maturity, we take the step into a new stage of life that will tax us in unexpected ways. We will then, however, look towards a potential spouse with different eyes; we will look for a similar level of maturity in the other. It takes two to marry and it takes maturity of commitment – commitment to stay with the marriage and commitment to examine oneself with openness towards the growth that the marriage union will call forth. Immaturity in marriage will manifest itself as escape, either from the marriage itself or from the growth that it seems to impose on us. Thus, commitment and the readiness to confront difficulties (which often equates to confronting our own egos) are perhaps the primary requisites of marriage, both for our own selves and for our future spouse. To me, this is summed up most poignantly in the simple words of the Bahá'í wedding vow: 'We will all, verily, abide by the will of God.' To be committed to abide by the will of God means, in part, that we are open to life – all that it offers, all that it presents to us. In this light, we recognize that the primal urge to escape goes against the very purpose of our being here.

The level of maturity required for us to really see ourselves and to discern the maturity level of a potential mate necessitates a more in-depth look at the dynamics of escape. The escape reflex is often unconscious; it exists within us, often operating and influencing us in significant ways without our being aware of it. For this reason the whole of the next chapter will be devoted to this subject as a necessary preliminary to being ready to step out and find a partner.

5

Escape

· · · · · · · · · ·

*All the best stories in the world are but one story in reality –
the story of an escape.
It is the only thing which interests us all and at all times,
how to escape.*

A. C. Benson

· · · · · · · · · ·

When we look at our lives from a spiritual perspective, when we
acknowledge that our lives have a spiritual purpose, we
eventually become aware that this presents a challenge which
never really leaves us. At those times when our soul's longing and
our ego's desires coincide, we experience a unity of being that
encourages us on our spiritual path. However, our ego's desires
rarely coincide with our soul's desires without conscious attention
and prayer. The development of a sense of self is a momentous step
for each human. We need a self in order to strive, make choices, and
fully exist as human beings. But once the self comes into being, it
tends to attach itself to material appetites which are beyond
appeasement. This is referred to in the Bahá'í writings as the
'persistent self'. Without spiritual direction and recognition of our

soul's longings, we are quite capable of – even likely to – get lost in this maze of material pursuit which is both endless and a dead-end at the same time. I want, first, to explain this essentially psychological form of escape a little more fully, then later I will explain why and how it relates to finding a marriage partner.

Escape into materialism

• • • • • • • • • •

The one with the most toys wins.

Bumper sticker

• • • • • • • • • •

Material pursuit in lieu of spiritual goals is in itself a massive form of escape or evasion of our true purpose. That is, when we do not even recognize our spiritual purpose, our whole life becomes a kind of escape. It may seem that, at times, even without spiritual direction, we do things that our egos would rather not do, like work instead of play, but this is usually only because our ego has temporarily postponed gratification so that it can later be gratified in a 'bigger' way: a larger TV, a bigger car, a drinking binge at the weekend, a more exotic vacation during our holiday time. If our life is mainly about material pursuit, our marriage will become just an extension of this pursuit and our marital relationship will simply be annexed by our ego's desires. In this state, no lasting fulfilment is ever achieved. The one with the most toys may win, but the prize is vacuity.

But the ego does not relinquish its passions even when it chooses a spiritual path. It is always ready to kick in, especially when we encounter difficulties on our path. When the going gets tough, when we encounter frustrations, our ego seeks escape. Thus escape, in an endless number of guises, is an almost constant attraction. Now, to someone who sees life from a spiritual point of view, marriage is also a spiritual institution. Rather than being something to pamper or glorify our egos, it is a process wherein our egos can learn submission and our souls can grow. Nevertheless, the desire to escape never leaves us completely.

In a way, our egos give up a lot when we choose to marry. We will be with the partner we choose rather than a potentially endless number of partners. We will have children who will require our support and for whom we will relinquish many freedoms. Yet a marriage that works well reaps spiritual dividends for both the married couple and the children they raise. But even in healthy marriages there are forms of escape which indulge our ego.

Escape within marriage

In marriage, the major form of escape is separation or divorce. Even when we marry with spiritual motivations, this major route of escape can often become a tantalising prospect. Frustrations, seemingly insoluble conflicts, can give rise to even more extreme yearnings to escape: suicide or even murder! But in fact, the spiritual demands of two different people, with different desires, propensities, interests and personalities, with huge responsibilities on their shoulders, living in close proximity, give rise to a huge and creative array of more subtle forms of escape. Couples can find ways of avoiding each other, avoiding responsibility, avoiding meeting challenges, avoiding true intimacy, in a staggering variety of ways. Many of these ways of escape are obviously unhealthy or immoral, like becoming addicted to something (the number of possible things humans can become addicted to is also astounding) or having an affair. Some forms of escape may seem quite innocuous, like playing golf, going fishing, playing bingo, constantly going out, or constantly staying home. Some means of escape can even appear to be virtuous, like focusing on the children, working overtime, keeping the house spotlessly clean. But all of these are often some form of escape. A marriage which is failing is one where escape has become a pattern.

Escape in life

• • • • • • • • • •

On the keyboard of life,
always keep one finger on the escape key.

Internet graffiti

• • • • • • • • • •

Now, why am I discussing escape in marriage when most of you reading this may not even have found a partner? Because the tendency to escape in marriage is related to the tendency to escape in life in general. Let me try to explain by breaking down the course of an intimate relationship into three phases: the pre-romantic, the romantic, and the post-romantic.

If I have caught you soon enough, you are still at the pre-romantic stage. The greater part of a marriage, providing the marriage is one that lasts, is post-romantic. This does not mean there is no romance in marriage, although sadly this is often the case. A healthy marriage has romance but romance is not the defining quality of the relationship. What I mean when I talk about the romantic phase of a relationship is that period when a couple are lost in their image of each other. (For a more complete explanation of romantic love see Chapter 9, 'Falling in Love'.) The pre-romantic phase is that stage of a relationship when one still has possession of one's faculties of discernment. Some people never have a pre-romantic phase: they are either not interested in a person or they are head over heels in love. Such individuals may seem to be having fun but they do not have successful relationships.

During the romantic phase of a relationship people may perform magnificently. In fact, it is quite amazing the way character can present itself when one is in love. But during this phase, one's discernment I.Q. hovers somewhere near 0. On the other hand, the learning that can take place in the pre-romantic phase, as we shall see in the next chapter, can tell us quite a lot about how our partner will be in the all-important post-romantic phase. This potential for learning during the pre-romantic phase can be enhanced if we create conditions during this phase which in some way match the conditions of post-romantic marriage. Let me explain.

One of the important features of a successful marriage is the ability to wake up to, and then close, escape routes that become routine. It is therefore important when looking for a partner and getting to know them, to be awake to escape routes and make every effort to carry on getting to know the other with the escape hatches closed. Although escape mechanisms exist both before marriage and after, they have a somewhat necessarily different character. For example, couples who have had a long relationship before they got married, perhaps even if they were living together before marriage, usually discover that being married is somehow different from not being married. Before being married, they could go somewhere else when there was tension or an argument. An initial feeling after marriage is often that there is nowhere to go – they are together and they are expected to stay together. It is only after encountering this feeling of being 'captured' that married people start to devise their creative means of escaping. But before marriage, the greatest form of escape is in not getting married. Sometimes this avoidance is because of a more or less conscious fear of getting married, more often it is disguised in some form of rationalization: 'I'm not the marrying type,' 'Marriage is just a piece of paper, if you really love someone you don't need it;' and so on. Some of these rationalizations can get quite involved – some become book-length and even get published!

This form of escape is more a tendency for men than for women. It may seem obvious to say, but a man who is still stuck in this form of escape is not a good candidate as a partner until he has changed his mindset, no matter how fine he may seem as a person. Men like this should not be pulled or lured into marriage, or even a close relationship, but need – of their own volition – to acknowledge and renounce this escape route.

But not wanting to get married is not the only form of escape for single people. Remembering that escape patterns make for troubled marriages, we should be aware of all manner of escape ploys before we become 'hooked' – this includes our own methods as well as those of any potential partner. The following section includes a number – though by no means all – of signs of escape, with some further explanations.

· · · · · · · · · ·

All men should try to learn before they die
what they are running from, and to, and why.

James Thurber

· · · · · · · · · ·

Signs of escape

· · · · · · · · · ·

Maturity: It's when you stop doing the stuff you
have to make excuses for
and when you stop making excuses for the stuff you have to do.

Marilyn Vos Savant

· · · · · · · · · ·

Drugs and alcohol

Recreational drug use and drinking alcohol are forms of escape. Many maintain that moderate use of marijuana or alcohol is relaxing, a healthy way of relieving stress. While it is true that most – if not all – of us struggle to handle the stresses of modern life, the way we approach this challenge is important. The use of substances like drugs and alcohol are a kind of short cut to addressing the larger issues of life-style which are at the heart of stress management problems. What are we doing? What choices are we making? What issues are we avoiding? What do we fear? Is there a lack of balance in our life-style? These are the important questions we should be asking ourselves with respect to stress management. Turning to drugs or alcohol, even in so-called moderation, is really just a seemingly easy way out of these more fundamental issues. Habitual or abusive use of drugs and alcohol are even more obvious means of escape but even these need to be addressed here, because of our great tendency to rationalize our actions or excuse them on the grounds that 'everybody does it'. First of all, not everybody does it. Second, even though these practices are unfortunately wide-spread, this is no excuse. We should learn to be our own person, and refusing these forms of escape is a good step towards really learning what we are made of. Getting drunk is becoming an ever more wide-spread feature of young people's social life, but getting drunk – even once – is really an extreme action. Flooding our whole bodies with a proven cell poison, affecting our ability to think and reason, puts our whole being into a compromise which could lead us, potentially, to do almost anything, and not even be aware of it.

Obsessions

• • • • • • • • • •

Anybody who watches three games of football in a row
should be declared brain dead.

Erma Bombeck

• • • • • • • • • •

Obsessions are all forms of escape. Obsessions with TV and video games are probably the most widespread; a huge amount of time is wasted in connection with these media. True, not **all** the time is wasted. We may learn and become informed through TV, and we may develop some moderately significant skills while playing computer games. They provide some recreational value, and we can turn to them for these reasons, but overdoing it – which most of us are wont to do – is a form of escape. Similarly, sports can be very invigorating and healthy, but being obsessed with them turns their virtue into loss.

Irresponsibility

Irresponsibility is another fundamental behavioural flaw, and it takes many forms. Are we working to build a useful life, developing useful skills which take discipline? Do we respect society's laws or, when we do not agree with them, do we show our disagreement in a responsible way? These are questions which help to bring one's degree of responsibility into focus.

Unresolved conflicts

Unresolved conflicts represent unfinished business. Especially when they concern our parents, they will enter into our future marriages. Conflicts can be very difficult to resolve, and can take a long time, but at the very least we should be awake to them, and on the path of resolving them and being willing to talk about them openly. Anything short of this does not auger well for our ability to face the demands that marriage presents.

Sex

Sexual intercourse is, in its most human form, a powerful and profound expression of intimacy, love and commitment. It can be – and sadly, often is – used in many other ways, each of which becomes another form of escape from our true self. When we use sex in other than its highest expression, we actually wound our ability to be true lovers. How this is so is a very large question which I shall devote a whole chapter to later on in this book.

Outer locus of control or aimlessness

Aimlessness, or following our parents', peers', or anyone else's agenda, often go hand in hand. We have already seen that one of our distinguishing features as humans is finding our purpose and pursuing goals. If we are not doing this, we are escaping. We are responsible for our own choices and should not give this sovereign territory over to anyone. Even our parents, who in our early years may in a way represent God and who have the grave responsibility of overseeing our development in our formative years, should not determine what we ultimately do with our lives. Again, consultation with others and especially with our parents can be very helpful, but our life is ultimately our own. Rebelling against our parents' wishes, however, is really just another way of giving them control. Both blindly living out the wishes of others, and wilfully going against them, are ways of giving them the power to set our agenda. We need to be beyond rebellion to see who we really are and to assess openly the possibilities before us.

Spiritual vacuum

A lack of spiritual awareness is one of the primary means of escape in these times. One of the reasons for this is that, for many, traditional religious institutions no longer represent spiritual authority. They may seem to be backward and old-fashioned, or they may appear to be just running to catch up with modern developments. But these often valid causes of turning away from religion do not relieve us of spiritual responsibility, nor of our soul's craving to know and love its Creator. Again, if we are turning away from this fundamental aspect of our human make-up, we are on the path of escape.

Self-centred/other-centred

Concern only with oneself, and concern only for others, are both examples of another two-sided coin which represents escape. We are not the centre of the universe, and part of being a developed human is to be awake to the needs and feelings of others. On the other hand, if our only cues to action are in response to others, we are giving up an inner call. While it is true that self-sacrifice is an important virtue to develop, we need to be sure there is a self there that is being given up!

Religious fanaticism

Fanaticism is another kind of obsession, but I am bringing it forward here because to the religious person it may just seem like the most needed kind of devotion. In reality, religious fanaticism is just another way of closing our eyes and giving over our responsibility, or of feeling spiritually superior, a sure indication of spiritual decline and escape. Religious fanaticism stems from a deep-seated feeling of insecurity; it can be likened to using religious teaching as a drug that can give an elevated sense of power. In this case, the source can be good but our take on it – or the take of others who are influencing us – is too one-sided. There are whole religious groups or denominations that are fanatical. They use the seeming need for followers to protect themselves from the secular or misguided world as a rationalization for closing minds. Opening our minds may expose us to many dangers but a closed mind is the most dangerous of all.

Homeless/homebound

Being either homeless or homebound are signs that we have given over something fundamental. To be married is to found a home with one's spouse. To enter into this stage of life, we should come from a home. If we have no home, we are in a way a lost soul and will not be really ready to make a home. Conversely, if we are too stuck in our family home, we do not show the preparedness to step out and make a home with another.

This list is by no means complete, yet it may seem as though I have already eliminated every potential mate from the planet. Luckily, this is not the case. Escape behaviour, as long as it is not an addiction, can be changed. When it is an addiction, it needs to be faced and overcome. Most of us may have gone through some of these behaviours – but that is just it, we should go **through** them and come out, more awake, on the other side. If we are thinking about marriage then we are considering embarking on an adult venture of the most demanding sort. We will need to face ourselves and our responsibilities and have a partner willing to do the same.

If you recognize signs of escape in someone you are attracted to but who has lots of endearing traits, I would counsel a healthy wariness. It is not wise to marry 'potential' with a view to changing your partner. On the other hand, it can be well worth confronting the other and discussing what you see. The pre-romantic stage is probably the best time for this because during romance your partner usually takes on an aura of near perfection, while during the post-romantic period you are more or less stuck with your investment – if some time after you are married your partner digs in his or her heels and you have never broached the issues beforehand, your options will be reduced and your resentments multiplied.

*** *** ***

Maturity might be defined as the state of taking responsibility for our choices and what follows from these choices. As children, we are guided by adults; as adolescents, we question those who have guided us and start to wonder what this is really all about. We have truly arrived at adulthood when we embrace the life that is given to us and take it on as our own, realizing that there is no one to answer to in our life save us. We are neither followers nor oppressed victims of circumstance looking for someone to blame for what happens to us. We echo the most profound utterance of the great prophets: 'Here am I.' The more consciously we do this, the more we rise to this level, the more we will be attracted to finding a partner who is also ready to face life with this maturity, knowing that in the course of our lives together, we will come face-to-face with our own fallibility and incompletely developed characters. We are not perfect souls looking for a perfect partner; rather, we are imperfect beings open to the perfecting processes of life and marriage, seeking a mate who will often be the one to provide those loving and painful occasions for our growth.

When on this path of search we come across souls we are attracted to, we need to be able to 'see' who they are. Bahá'u'lláh has said that the seeker should 'so cleanse his heart that no remnant of either love or hate may linger therein, lest that love blindly incline him to error, or that hate repel him away from the truth.' Thus, seeing requires detachment, and attraction can be one of the greatest barriers to seeing. This, then, brings us to the next phase of our quest: the period of observation, where our ability to see will be put to the test.

6

Observation and Inventory

Being single and unattached can be a very productive time. Even if we do not feel we are ready to find a partner and enter into the courtship period we can, through developing platonic friendships with members of the opposite sex, learn much about what kind of person we are comfortable with and also about the foolishness of judging a book by its cover. We can have our eyes open to people, observe how couples interact, learn from the mistakes others make as they jump into relationships and get hurt and, overall, just become good observers of human qualities. When we do feel it is time in our life to start taking seriously the prospects of finding a mate, we can still use the period of being unattached to good advantage.

What kind of partner do we want?

It is a very good idea, before we actually start to 'test' the field, to develop a clear idea of the kind of partner we want. This is a process which takes some introspection and also consultation with others. Both, in my opinion, are important. Everyone is different. We all have our peculiar tastes, attractions, and needs. What is good for one person may not be at all good for another.

Thus, we need to go inside and reflect upon the qualities that are most important for us in a future partner. It is good to be as conscious as possible in doing this, writing down the qualities and giving the reasons we believe these qualities are important. We should also write down the traits we could not bear in a partner and give reasons for these.

Talking to others, especially people whose experience we value, and discussing this topic of qualities to look for, can help us put our own idiosyncratic tastes and desires into perspective. People who have good and bad experience in relationships, especially couples who have had healthy enduring marriages, can give many useful pointers about what works – and what doesn't work – and such input may bring us to revise our list of what we are looking for.

Some think that we should develop as comprehensive list as possible for the kind of partner we want. This may be a good idea, but I would suggest that, if we are going to include a detailed profile of our future partner, we should be ready to do some revision when we actually start to meet potential partners. A detailed list should also be prioritized. What qualities are the most important, what qualities are not nearly so important? We should be clear on this. The most important component of any such list is to have two or three essential qualities we are looking for. These are qualities that we would not want to compromise under any circumstances. It may take some time and consultation to gain clarity on this.

Someone similar or someone different?

When looking for a partner, should we find someone who is like us or someone who is opposite? Research has found that similarities are important. If we are going to spend our life with someone and raise a family with that person we should want to be with that kind of person. It is quite possible to fall in love with someone who is not the kind of person we like to be with, or who is not a good candidate for marriage. Differences between people, when they have to live together day after day, year after year, making crucial life decisions together, weathering the battles of life together, can become confounding sources of trouble. Just a seemingly small difference, such as what temperature to keep the house, can and has been the main cause for couples to divorce (this shouldn't happen, but it does)! Imagine how more significant differences will be difficult to manage on a regular basis.

Neil Clark Warren, who describes similarities as assets and differences as debts, gives special mention to four of each which he thinks are most critical. The most essential similarities, according to him, have to do with intelligence, values, interests and expectations about roles. The four differences likely to cause the most friction in marriage, in his view, have to do with energy level, personal habits (like punctuality, cleanliness, smoking), money, and verbal inclinations. These are not rules, but these kinds of similarities can make marriages easier, while the difficulties can rob the couple of the comfort and ease most of us expect within the home.

Finding a balance

On the question of differences, two divergent perspectives seem evident. One informs us of our natural desire to feel comfortable with the partner we want to share a life with and, for this, similar tastes, habits, capacities, values, cultural background, financial status, and interests are helpful. The other reminds us that marriage is itself founded upon the already different natures of man and woman coming together, and that forming unity with diverse elements is the keynote of human relationships and needs, especially at this time.

These two seemingly disparate truths are both in their own way correct, yet neither is sufficient as a basis for choice. In conscious courtship, I suggest we be alert to both realities and seek a healthy balance. In the process of seeking out the essential qualities of humans, the period of being unattached can be very useful. By learning the art of observation, and looking at inner human qualities, we can develop a much sounder basis for choice.

Cross-cultural marriages

One difference that usually signals a whole range of differences has to do with ethnicity. The difference between people of different cultural backgrounds is usually very significant along a wide variety of measures. Does this mean we should avoid marrying someone from another culture? The fact is, people of widely divergent backgrounds are coming together to form families more and more often. In the Bahá'í teachings, marrying someone from a different race or ethnic origin is seen as one of the ways of promoting unity in the world. However, these facts do not make intercultural marriages easy. We need to look at this with our eyes wide open, and in doing so we will learn much more about what it takes to live in the modern world and have a successful marriage. This will lead us to developing a more healthy perspective on differences in general.

We may want to challenge ourselves by finding somebody who is from a very different economic background, who is intellectually at a very different level, or who is from a different culture or race. Sometimes searching for these factors is motivated by romantic notions. But if we are going to marry someone from a different ethnic group or a different part of the world, do we know them and their world well? Many people of European background have very romantic notions about people from other cultures, whether Africans, Asians, native Americans, Aborigines or Roma. We need to go far beyond this superficial level before we are ready to consider marrying someone from such a different background.

But more likely is a tendency to harbour deep-seated prejudices towards people of very different backgrounds, prejudices which our liberal consciousness tends to deny. These issues should be explored and resolved, **before** they become factored into a romance.

• • • • • • • • • •

There is so much to be said for exotic marriages.
If your husband is a bore,
it takes years longer to discover.

Saul Bellow

• • • • • • • • • •

Dangers in similarities

It **is** easier to have a happy marriage with someone who is more like you, but there are dangers in this too. If a couple are very similar to each other they may get along well, but in their orientation to the outside world they may be missing out on a lot. The more similar two people are in a marriage, the more likely they will have blind spots concerning character, or prejudices which because of their similarities may not be adequately confronted. One of the reasons cross-cultural marriages are encouraged in the Bahá'í teachings is that the Bahá'í vision for the world is unity in diversity; and marriage, being the foundation of society, is also a sign of unity in diversity. In other words, when we marry, a man and a woman come together with all their differences and build a mini-world through their family. The capacities that are developed in this process are extended into the world, helping us to live with wider differences within our wider community. Now that the world has contracted into a global village, the family circle itself can be a source of insight if couples take on the challenge of cross-cultural marriages and learn to make them work.

Developing spiritual capacity

I am myself a great fan of cross-cultural marriages because my own wife and I come from opposite sides of the planet and very different cultures. But I am aware of the fact that many cross-cultural marriages fail and that they do take generally more effort. Again, we need to have our eyes open as much as possible to what we are taking on when we marry. But here I want to bring forward a point that I believe to be an important ingredient in all marriages, indeed, to all human relationships. We need to be open to change and willing to stretch ourselves to learn what our capacities really are. Our egos are prone to self-centredness and a feeling of supremacy, both of which tend to make them resistant to wanting to learn from others and to change. But spiritually speaking, we are not here to heed our egos, but to grow as God created us to grow. Encountering difference in the close quarters of marriage is difficult, but insofar as we are able to stretch ourselves and respectfully understand the wants of our partner, we grow spiritually and realize more and more of our human potential. Life, moreover, is about change. We change, our partners change, our circumstances change. Developing the capacity to willingly stretch ourselves is a useful proactive stance to the inevitability of change.

Some factors of difference bring up questions of a spiritual nature, or bring us into the sphere where only by looking at things from a spiritual point of view can we find a resolution. For example, is it important to find someone who is from a well-off family, or who is already making a good income? If we are accustomed to a materially comfortable lifestyle, it is going to be a challenge to live otherwise. However, it may be a good challenge. If we can truly have our eyes open, both to the ways we will be challenged **and** to the spiritual blessings of developing detachment from worldly goods, then we are in a better position to make a healthy choice about looking seriously at a potential partner who does not offer much materially. On a practical level, **how** money is viewed and handled by each partner is almost sure to be an issue, so this needs to be explored thoroughly and looked at very soberly.

· · · · · · · · ·

Like dear St Francis of Assisi I am wedded to Poverty;
but in my case the marriage is not a success.

Oscar Wilde

· · · · · · · · ·

Of all the similarities that are important, probably the most important is the need to share similar values. Our ability to choose is intrinsic to our being and therefore the moral ground we choose to stand on is deeply significant. Remember, human beings are moral creatures. There are many animals that are social animals, but what holds them together is programmed into them. Humans, on the other hand, are held together through moral agreement. If we disagree on the level of what we value, then unity is not really possible.

Religious differences

• • • • • • • • • •

Does being born into a Christian family make one a
Christian?
No! God has no grandchildren.

Corrie ten Boom

• • • • • • • • • •

Since religion usually has a lot to do with what is valued, most say it is important to find someone who shares your fundamental beliefs. This can be true, but not necessarily. Not everyone who identifies with a particular religion holds it to be equally significant in their lives – the depth of commitment of one may be very different from another. How many people are there in the world who identify themself with this or that religion – even attend collective worship on a regular basis – yet live a life ruled more profoundly by material concerns? In fact, materialism – although it is void of meaning – is the dominant religion of the world today, despite the fact that most of its adherents do not identify their god as being money or pleasure.

However, where religious identification also entails true devotion and commitment, it becomes crucial to find unity on these elements. On one level we all have a different religion, because we all understand and interpret the teachings given to us in our Holy Books in our own unique way and act according to our own understanding. On another level, religion comes from our Creator, who is One, and we who are God's conscious creatures should be able to find agreement on how to bring this forward into our collective lives. This certainly includes having a vision of how we will live out our faith in our family. In the societies of the Western world, where individuality is so highly prized, religion is also often seen as being just another matter of individual choice. But religion is really the basis by which we learn to live together and realize our unity. Religion is also a life philosophy giving direction to our lives and setting priorities. In marriage, we want to be moving in the same direction. Religion influences our relation to the outside world in other significant ways. Thus, we will really need the capacity to explore this issue openly and deeply, and come to agreement.

Avoiding rigidity

If we develop too rigid an idea of the kind of person we want to marry, we may miss out on some very good potential partners. Sometimes we want in a partner what we do not want to develop in ourselves. For example, many males are raised in households where the females – usually the mother but sometimes even a sister or sisters – take care of all domestic duties. This is obviously a very comfortable position for males who are able to eat but need not worry about cooking, who make messes but don't have to concern themselves with cleaning up, and who read newspapers or watch sports while females are busy keeping the house tidy and the children looked after. Boys brought up in this kind of environment tend to expect and look for a female partner who will continue in their mother's shoes. Many women, especially in the West, are waking up to the injustice that is usually inherent in these situations and are developing other aspects of themselves and, along with these, other expectations from a male partner. If males want to continue in the traditional path of domestic comfort – as many do – they have to look farther and farther afield for a partner. Indeed, there are men who look for wives from East Asia, believing and expecting that these women will look after them like their mothers did! A more healthy orientation is to look at this as a challenge to develop a greater sense of responsibility for the home environment and the raising of children and to develop a side of ourselves that has been neglected.

Observation

· · · · · · · · · ·

I think men who have a pierced ear are better prepared for marriage.
They've experienced pain and bought jewellery.

Rita Rudner

· · · · · · · · · ·

All of the foregoing discussion has to do with gaining clarity on what we are looking for in a spouse. We need to use this clarity for what we are looking for and develop the ability to see the character of others. We do not do this to judge others; passing judgement is the work of God. We do it in order to discern who we might be ready to raise a family with. At this stage, all this is accomplished without having become involved with anyone.

A very common pattern in Western society's culture of relationships is to let someone know you are interested in them as soon as you feel an attraction. This takes place in many forms. Usually the man approaches the woman, making it obvious that he is attracted to her and intends to get to know her better. However, we also find more and more women approaching men for the same purpose. The environment in which such an approach takes place often leads to certain conclusions. For example, if a man approaches a woman he has never seen in his life before, in a dance club for instance, both will already know that he is attracted to her, so she either accepts his approach or refuses. This move by the man will usually expose her interest or lack of interest in him. Body language and verbal communication will let the other person know if there is an attraction present from her side or not. In a very short period of time, without either the man or woman having any real idea what the other is like, both of them will have laid their cards on the table.

• • • • • • • • • •

Once the toothpaste is out of the tube, it is awfully hard to get it back in.

H. R. Haldeman

• • • • • • • • • •

We can make a conscious effort to avoid falling into this pattern. First of all, we have developed some ideas of what we want in a partner. Since it is very possible, for a variety of reasons, to feel attracted to someone who does not have some of the traits that are important to us, it makes sense to step back and compare the one who attracts us to the inventory we have developed. Secondly, there are many things we can learn by taking our time and observing someone before getting involved with them. Looking at it the other way around, there are many things we will not 'see' in another person as soon as we get involved with them. Also, as soon as the other person senses there is an attraction, their behaviour is likely to change.

This kind of observation phase works best in group settings. In groups we can see how a person relates to others, how much their behaviour is geared to gaining attention, how they communicate, how interested they are in people regardless of looks or status. If we have the opportunity to see a person around children, we can often get an idea of their abilities and interests in this area.

Observing friendships

One area important to observe in another is how they are with friends and what kind of friends they keep. It is possible to learn a lot through observing friendship patterns and it is also possible to discreetly get to know the friends of the one you may be interested in, in order to get to know more about him or her. What the friends are like and how you feel about them may tell you something about the person. What his or her friends say about the friendship can also be revealing.

Service

· · · · · · · · · ·

No person was ever honoured for what he received;
honour has been the reward for what he gave.

Calvin Coolidge

· · · · · · · · · ·

We can gain even deeper impressions of people when we witness them in the context of service projects. Here, the demands on people are greater and we can observe qualities on more levels. How steadfast is a person when the going gets tough? How well do they work with others? How do they deal with conflict? How able are they to contribute to problem solving? How well have they developed the art of consultation? All of these are most helpful in learning about another, and all of them can change as soon as an attraction is made known. Besides this, being involved in service projects is intrinsically good for us, and the fact of getting involved says something in itself.

Love at first sight

Interestingly, both in Western and Eastern societies, the period when a couple can really come to know each other is timed to occur once they are both emotionally or socially committed to each other. In the West, most people somehow think that there must be love at first sight, or that they will find the right partner by trial and error. In the traditional East, marriage partners are usually either chosen by the parents or family considerations or the man appears from out of nowhere and proposes.

The Western paradigm goes something like this:

1. attraction

2. sex

3. get to know your partner

In the East it is more like this:

1. proposal

2. marriage

3. get to know your spouse

In both cases, really getting to know your partner is pushed to third place either by sex or by marriage itself – two very powerful forces, each of which are irreversible events. The scheme that is proposed here in a simplified form shows us a very different pattern:

1. attraction

2. get to know your potential partner from a distance

3. get to know your partner up close with gradually more emotional involvement

4. proposal

5. marriage

6. continued development and progress towards unity.

But what about love at first sight? I am not denying that such a phenomenon exists. Nor am I suggesting that when it occurs it is always misleading or likely to end up in disaster. The 'chemistry' that can occur between a man and a women when they first meet can be powerful indeed. A review of some of the points made in the chapter on attraction may be in order here. When we feel very strong initial attraction we should first and foremost be awake to the possibility of it being purely sexual. Beyond this, there exists the very real possibility that you have found an Imago match (see pages 78–80 for an explanation of Imago). If this is the case, the question to ask yourself is if you are ready and prepared to take steps toward marriage and, equally important, if the one you are attracted to has reached that stage of development. This is where detachment is called for, and consultation with others who are more able to view both of you with objectivity and wisdom.

Two things about Imago matchings are worth bringing up at this point. The first is this: when Imago match-ups are involved, the initial attraction is just the tip of the iceberg. In time, the two lovers are going to confront their shadow selves in each other, and conflicts will touch upon forgotten and repressed feelings from their childhood. It takes commitment, openness, and maturity to work through these entangled and unconscious episodes. Secondly, while the matching of Imagos is a very selective process, there are very definitely many more individuals out there who match up to your Imago. You will have other chances.

It should be clarified here that, in the above scheme, the longest premarital stage is stage 3. The observation from afar phase is only the relatively brief period before any overture or expression of interest is made known. Once this step has been taken, a longer and more serious period of getting to know the other is envisioned. This very important stage will be covered in Chapter 8 on courtship. But next on our agenda is to look more carefully at the exciting step that leads to courtship.

7

Advances

Let us say – however unlikely this may be – that you not only agree with most of what has been said up to now, but that you have even put the ideas into practice. This means that you have advanced to the stage where you have observed potential mates from a distance and got a good, objective feel for what kind of person they are. If you have really done this well you have almost surely run across very good candidates who, for one reason or another, you have believed to be unsuitable as a marriage partner. But let us say that you have actually encountered one who not only attracts you but seems to fit your bill. What next?

The next step is indeed a momentous one and needs to be discussed quite fully, even though the step itself may only take a matter of minutes. What I am talking about, of course, is making an advance – making your interest known, so that the two of you (providing the one in your sights is willing) can take more serious steps towards getting to know one another. If we are alive, and if we are human, this is quite rightfully an anxious moment. A lack of anxiety at such a time would probably betray a lack of serious intent or interest.

It is time to pause, take a breath, and look at a few critical questions. Who should make the advance? How should the advance be made? What is the content of our invitation; in other words, what exactly is it that we want of the next step we are initiating? If someone we are interested in makes an advance towards us, how should we receive it? Finally, if someone we are clearly not interested in makes an advance towards us, how do we decline? Some of these questions may sound trivial or simply common sense, but they are not. This is a critical juncture on the path to marriage and should be handled with as much conscious-ness as we can muster, so let us proceed to address these questions in order.

Who should make the advance?

Traditionally, in the vast majority of cultures, the male has been the one to take the steps to initiate courtship – that is, in cultures where others are not involved in arranging the marriage. Nowadays the picture is not nearly so clear. First of all, the making of advances today rarely has anything to do with marriage. Advances are made in order to strike up a relationship, or even just to have some fun. And even when the intent is towards a serious relationship or marriage, the field is wide open to both males and females. It is no longer expected that the female demurely wait, even if she is very interested in a man, while the man plucks up the courage to make his intentions known, if, indeed, he has any intentions. While it may have been difficult for interested males to find the courage, it was probably even more difficult for the female who just had to wait.

There are, to be sure, many who still tend toward the traditional pattern, but there are a growing number who do not feel at all bound by it. In fact, there is a trend for females to openly show their interest in males they are attracted to, and a matching pattern for many males to passively let the females take the lead, to let them do the pursuing. To many, this is just another manifestation of the equality of the sexes taking hold – a correction to the imbalances of the past and of previous rigidity in gender roles.

My own view on this is that because every situation is unique and personalities can vary to huge degrees, there need to be allowances for these idiosyncrasies and a certain amount of flexibility. Having said this, however, there are psychological reasons – even anthropological reasons – for maintaining the traditional pattern as the norm. Let us explore some of these.

I have already stressed that, in what has been frivolously called the mating game, the emotional and psychological stakes are very high. It is very easy for a couple to come together, but **staying** together is quite another matter. Even when emotionally healthy individuals come together and allow themselves to be intimate and truly close, if they break up the resulting separation can really hurt and wound. In this respect, the emotional stakes are more or less equal for men and women, except that men are often more prone to be sexually schizoid – that is, males have more of a tendency to disconnect their feeling self from their sexual self and to view sexual intercourse as an encounter or game, rather than an expression of intimacy (for more on this see Chapter 10 on sex).

In another respect, the emotional and social stakes are much higher for the woman than for the man. This stems from the most deeply significant difference between the sexes: the fact that it is the woman who bears children. Looking at this from an evolutionary perspective, the longer a creature has to care for its young before they gain independence, the more important it is for the mother to find a secure environment in which to bear and nurture the offspring. There is no creature that takes anywhere near as much care, time, attention, and resourcefulness to raise its young as do human beings. The more humans have developed as a species, the more this has become the case. Even in recent history this continues to be the trend: the time span, consciousness and resources put into the rearing of children have increased with each succeeding generation.

Despite this trend of an increasing need for security and resources for the human child, the biological fact of carrying, bearing, and shouldering the greater part of the responsibility of looking after the child remains with the mother. The only balancing factor in this very unbalanced scenario is the commitment of the mother's mate to be there to support this huge undertaking, and for legal and religious institutions to remind men to share and play their rightful role in this venture. With the demise and waning of religious institutions, civil law has had to take up the slack. But the fact remains that if the man's own sense of commitment is lacking, the forces of society – of even the most enlightened societies in the world – ultimately fall short in adequately compensating for any man who does not take ownership of his responsibility as a mate and father.

One well-known feminist has said that the sexual revolution was not a feminist revolution. One of her main reasons for saying this is the fact that one of the results of so-called sexual liberation has been a huge number of single mothers. In this respect, women are generally the losers. While there are many wonderful exceptions, the frequent profile of a single mother is that of a person with less free time, more frustration, more tiredness and lower self-esteem than her peers, who is lower on the social and financial scale and has seemingly fewer choices in life. Even more important is the situation of children who are brought up in a single-parent household. Many lack a bond with the father, often scrambling for his attention, often taking their frustration out on the mother for the father's lack of being there. These children often lack an adequate adult male role model and are often presented with a haggard female role model. We know that homes where mother and father are present and responsible are still never perfect, but overall the single-parent family (and the great majority of single-parent families are mother-parent families) is not a wholesome or complete one.

With this social and evolutionary background, my main point can now be made: since women are, practically speaking, destined to shoulder huge responsibility in intimate relationships and the man's role is much more voluntary, at the stage of courtship the woman should do her utmost to be assured that she finds a man who will go the distance with her. If the female is the one who has to chase down the male at the outset of their relationship, she deprives herself of the opportunity to see if this man is – **of himself** – really interested in her. Moreover, she may also be depriving the man of this opportunity to take stock of his interest!

• • • • • • • • • •

Jerry had never done anything he wanted
since he had married her,
and he hadn't really wanted to do that.

Kate Douglas

• • • • • • • • • •

When there are trials in a marriage, we inevitably ask ourselves, 'Do I really want this?' When this critical question comes up – and I am speaking more for men here than for women – we need to be able to go back to the relationship's genesis and say, 'Although this is a really difficult situation for me, **I chose it**. I have to do everything I can to see it through and, in any case, give my family all the support they need.' If we are the ones who took the first difficult steps and continued to persevere and take the lead in the courtship process, we are more likely to take ownership for the relationship, to be steadfast when the going gets tough and to face up to the most difficult issues.

There are other psychological factors bearing on the question of who should make the initial advance. First of all, females tend to be much more aware of the early mating processes than males, probably because of the evolutionary influences mentioned above. I have heard very perceptive men acknowledge that even in traditional encounters where men are the pursuers, it is the women who orchestrate the whole scene and are in control. It is true and good that women often have this capacity, but it needs to be used with wisdom. In the many cases here in Europe where we have observed young couples in the early stages of courting, my wife has often pointed out to me how blank and unaware the faces of the young men are; they often seem to have no idea what they are doing or what they have got themselves into. In Hungary, where we live, the balance of power is much too much in the men's court and women feel they have to work extra hard to 'land' one. This is an extremely unhealthy situation for all parties. A woman needs to be in a position where she can use her wiles more in testing a man rather than landing him.

How to advance

· · · · · · · · · ·

Don't be afraid to take a big step if one is indicated.
you can't cross a chasm in two small jumps.

David Lloyd George

· · · · · · · · · ·

The other side of the coin is the difficulty men have in taking the first step. If a man is genuinely interested in a woman, he usually feels great trepidation in putting himself forward and inviting the woman to whom he is attracted to take a step – whatever that step may be – towards getting to know one another better. There are, of course, lots of men – let's call them predators – who just want a one-night stand or short-term encounters to gratify their sexual desires or appease their egos. These, because they have nothing emotional to invest, feel no qualms about making advances. The predator – partly because he is emotionally detached, and also because he gets more practice – often becomes very good at knowing what to say to 'get' a woman. One good reason for a woman to cultivate the art of observation and testing in the courtship phase is to protect herself from the predator. It helps if women are aware that there is a predator in most men – a side of them which just want to 'have' a woman. A higher motivation can be evoked in a man if the woman has the wherewithal to keep the predator at bay, to see it and confront it.

But back to the man who is in touch with a more genuine attraction. This man feels the stakes to be high; feels he is putting himself on the line; and feels the terrible fear that he may come face-to-face with rejection. This is the fellow whose hand shakes when he picks up the phone to call his potential loved one, who rehearses again and again what to say and how to say it. This is the one who goes through this process time after time before actually carrying it through. This is the man who stammers and stutters to get out his well-rehearsed lines. This is the hell that a good man must go through just for a chance to make a connection, but this is the least of what he must face in himself if he is to begin to prove himself worthy as a potential mate.

However great a test as this can be for a male of serious intent, the female's part is unquestionably more taxing. Her test is to learn patience with equanimity. While there are things she can do to catch a man's eye, men can be incredibly blind and caught up with other things. She must remember that the more she does to grab a response from the man, the more she is taking away from the man's duty to wake up and make a move. This may sound contrived or even manipulative, but in fact this is an ability which springs from an inner source that is in touch with the grave responsibility for children yet unborn.

The essence of a woman's task is to not let herself be pulled away from her own noble centre. This calls forth from the man an ability to show courage, humility and respect to the woman he would approach. If these complementary roles of man and woman sound like something out of King Arthur, there is truth in it, for they represent archetypes within us which are timeless. Courtship originated in the courts of nobles and monarchs. We are dealing with powerful energy and the only appropriate approach is a respectful one.

What do you want?

• • • • • • • • • •

Tell me about yourself – your struggles, your dreams, your telephone number.

Peter Arno

• • • • • • • • • •

And so it is my view – however archaic this may sound – that it is most appropriately the male who makes the initial move. Let me then follow through on how this scenario ideally unfolds; later I will approach the necessary question of female advances. Having illustrated the need for great respect and humility in the male's approach, let us clarify what exactly is to be accomplished in this forward advance. It should be clear by now that we are not playing around, that both parties have marriage ultimately in their sight and consciousness. If you have not yet bought into this view, the chapters on sexuality should go further towards clarifying this. But while marriage is ultimately the goal, what we want to achieve at this stage is simply to be able to get to know the other person better and to ask them if they are willing to take this step. The actual steps in getting to know the other better are covered in the next chapter; all that is needed here is agreement to move into this next phase.

Being clear on this last point can go a long way to relieving at least some of the stress that men feel when contemplating an advance. Being able to communicate that this is what you want can also go a long way in helping the woman towards whom you are making the advance. Chances are that by this point she too may be getting herself tied into a knot. The antithesis of this can be exemplified something like this: 'I love you. I want to marry you. You are the only one for me, the girl I have always been looking for. And if you refuse me I won't be able to take it. I will kill myself.' This is, of course, an extreme version of emotional blackmail, but it makes a point. The male needs to take ownership for his own feelings. If he has already allowed himself to fall head-over-heels in love, he needs to recognize that this is his own choice and take ownership of it rather than laying it on the other. The principle emphasized in the next chapter is to take it as cool as you can for as long as you can. You both will have a lot to learn about each other and learning does not take place when the emotional heat is turned up high.

Receiving an advance

· · · · · · · · · ·

Don't accept rides from strange men, and remember that all men are strange.

Robin Morgan

· · · · · · · · · ·

Now we need to turn to the woman who is receiving the advance from the man. She may have been hoping for such an opportunity for a long time, or she may be completely surprised and befuddled. In either case, excitement or wonderment, keeping a cool head and knowing what to do is almost impossible if there has not been some serious thinking about how to receive advances beforehand. This thinking includes anticipating as many situations as possible, deciding the kind of response you want to give in each. Let us look at a couple of possible scenarios.

First, the woman needs to look at how the advance is delivered. Is it respectful? Is it sincere? Or is it coercive, or arrogant? Is it too overdone, as in the example above? Let us assume that the man is actually someone that the woman is interested in but his approach is not respectful. In this case, despite the woman's interest, she does herself an injustice if she doesn't put the man in his place. No matter how much she may be attracted to him, a crisp way to send him back to the drawing board is called for. If this repulse sends him away, never to come back, he probably was not worth thinking about in the first place and nothing is lost. If, on the other hand, he licks his wounds, rethinks his approach, changes his attitude and comes back with an apology, then perhaps a beginning can be made.

• • • • • • • • • •

I asked this girl out and she said, 'You got a friend?' I said yes, she said, 'Then go out with him.'

Dom Irrera

• • • • • • • • • •

Let us say the woman finds the man interesting and worthy of attention **and** his approach to her is winning and respectful. Even here, there is no need for the woman to fall over backwards to make herself available. Balance and wisdom are called for, every step of the way. The male should not only be interested, but able to withstand some testing, but this may be quite a delicate operation. In my opinion, if he is left guessing to some degree about the woman's commitment to his offer, that is not bad at all. The woman should feel no compulsion to make a decision about the man's proposition right away.

It is good for a woman to look for some self-confident female role models and observe examples of responding that are healthy and fit their personality. Some examples can be found in novels, but it may take some looking, especially if your sources are contemporary. Elizabeth Bennet in Jane Austen's *Pride and Prejudice* is a classic example of a woman of substance and intelligence handling various pressures and proposals with dignity.

• • • • • • • • • •

Even when pursued,
the butterfly is never in a hurry.

Japanese proverb

• • • • • • • • • •

Declining

• • • • • • • • • •

*Nothing takes the taste out of peanut butter quite like
unrequited love.*

Charlie Brown

• • • • • • • • • •

If the man is not someone the woman is particularly attracted to, the
first thing to observe is still his style and attitude in approaching her.
If it is disrespectful, the woman need not feel too worried about
hurting his feelings. While there may be no need to pull punches
here, the woman is best advised to deliver her refusal as coolly as
possible, for any tinge of strong emotion can be interpreted as
interest by the suitor. It might help if we all learned some assertive-
ness techniques so as to find a clean and courteous way to ward off
advances we are not interested in, especially disrespectful ones.

If, however, the man is sincere and kind-hearted in his
approach, no matter how much the woman may **not** be interested
in him, her mode of declining should be as kind and empathetic as
possible without giving a double message. Being mean, or
stringing someone along, are not ways to respond to a soul, no
matter how unattractive he may be to you. Some women receive a
lot of pressured advances from a lot of men and tend to develop a
hard exterior, failing to recognize or develop appropriate
responses to more sensitive types. A woman needs to develop a
repertoire of appropriate responses. It never hurts to come up
with creative, on-the-spot responses; but to know you have a
repertoire to fall back on helps one to remain relaxed enough to
come up with more spontaneous replies.

A new role for men

Because so many women nowadays make advances towards men,
it has become as important for men to develop the ability to

decline these advances. This is **not** something men are socialized to do. It has been the expectation, in the past, that any overtures from women should be taken advantage of. A man declining a woman's advance has come to mean one of two things: either the woman is desperately unattractive to him, or he is gay and has no interest in women.

· · · · · · · · · ·

I came into my hotel room one night and found a strange blonde in my bed.
I would stand for none of that nonsense.
I gave her exactly twenty-four hours to get out.

Groucho Marx

· · · · · · · · · ·

Because males have not been socialized to decline female advances, there are almost no role models to refer to. The principles for declining advances are, however, the same as for women. If the woman's overtures are coarsely sexual she can be put in her place. If the interest she shows is sincere but you are not interested in her as a potential partner, a kind but deterrent approach is called for. If the advances persist, a more frank, to-the-point explanation is needed. This is a challenging area for men, but one in which we need to develop clarity and be prepared.

***   ***   ***

To sum up, I believe there are good psychological reasons for the burden of making an advance to fall most properly on the man. Similarly, how to receive the advance, and whether to accept the proposition put forward, ought most usually to be the prerogative of the woman. Both parties should have the long view in sight, but the short-term goal is to determine whether they are both ready and willing to take steps that may or may not get them closer to the long-term goal. The man must be ready to pursue, even if rebuffed; the woman must protect her ground and her dignity, for the opportunities for sizing up a man are more limited than one thinks, and the stakes for her are much, much higher. While it may not seem that there are many men out there ready to honour a woman, if a woman refuses to accept anything less than honour, then she may be surprised to find how many men are ready to become honourable. One side of men – i.e., their egos – hates to be rebuffed or forced to fall into line; another side – and this is archetypal – deeply respects a woman who feels her own dignity; men are then often ready to clean up their act in order to court this rare prize.

One more point before going on. The next chapter comprises primarily practical suggestions for young couples who are interested in getting to know each other better without diving headlong into love with each other. While the decision to do this is made after an advance is made, it is not a decision that one has to stick to through thick and thin. This is not yet marriage, by a long way. The woman especially should be wary, and if unhappy with the man's commitment to the process according to her liking, be ready to pull out. The man, I believe, should be kept in pursuit and the woman's attitude much like that before the advance. With this background, let us then move into the next phase and explore practical ways and places where couples can get to know each other's characters and tastes more thoroughly.

8

Courtship

Once the advance has been made and both parties agree to take steps to get to know each other better, we move into a new and crucial period. The urge to get to know a person for whom we feel an attraction and who possesses the qualities that are most important for us in a partner is natural. The more we know about another person we like, the more we want to know. Courtship, or dating, may be considered the most crucial period in the process of decision making about a partner. Getting to know a person in this way will lead a couple either to fall in love with each other or for one or the other (or both) to recognize that the other is not a good choice of partner and to bring the courtship period to a close. In the former case it may be of great advantage to both if falling in love occurs later rather than sooner, because the brain can still control the heart.

The process and the nature of 'falling in love' will be discussed in the next chapter. All that needs to be mentioned here is that with a clear head and clear heart one is in a better position to judge for oneself and be objective. I have divided the courtship period into two sections, a period before falling in love, and a period after falling in love. The line between the two is case-dependent but, as we shall see, also dependent upon our will and choice.

As implied in the last chapter, once the intent of the parties has been clarified it is much harder to remain clear-headed and objective. But this does not mean that we should throw out all objectivity and fall head over heels in love just because we know that the one whom we are attracted to is also interested in us. As previously suggested, the woman, in her attitude and demeanour, can prolong an ambiguous or conditional state of commitment to this process. This can help her test the man's mettle and sincerity. Playing it cool is a good way to get under a male's mask, for it is a challenge to his ego. It is true that certain feelings of togetherness feed the desire to let go, but the choices are still ours as to what we allow ourselves to share and do together. Falling in love is always ultimately a choice. If it seems that it isn't, it is only because we are either not paying attention to our inner processes or we are shirking irresponsibly.

While falling in love is primarily the subject of the next chapter, I want to emphasize this last point and make it as clear as possible: Falling in love is a choice! Without being clear on this, much of the remainder of this chapter won't make sense and can't be received with an open mind. I know that there are many dissenting voices to the seemingly unromantic statement that falling in love is a choice. Often these voices are singing, 'I can't help falling in love with you!' It's time for another case study.

Janice had been abused as a child and had endured a marriage where, in various ways, her husband's behaviour was irresponsible and betrayed a basic lack of respect. In the end, her husband left her but despite all the problems she had endured with him, her 'love' kept her attached and suffering for a long period. In a way, she clung to her feelings of 'love' as she had clung to her husband, yet neither were giving her much in return. She explained that, being a painter, this was her 'artist's heart', that if she didn't 'feel' in this way, her art would somehow not be as expressive.

I worked with her for part of this period, helping her work through her grief and also dealing with the issue of abuse in her background. She had a lot of capacity to grow and change, and worked through a lot of her painful past. Although she did not think anyone would be interested in her anyway, I did what I could to prepare her for future relationships. In fact she was a very attractive and talented woman.

After a period of not coming in for sessions, she again contacted me asking for an appointment. She had met a man who was really interested in her. She had, remembering my counsel, held him at arm's length for several months while he quite respectfully pursued her. Finally, she 'gave in' and for her there was no turning back, her 'artist's heart' had taken over. For him, however, as soon as this corner was turned, he suddenly realized that he had unresolved issues with a past girlfriend. He immediately became distant and stopped pursuing Janice. The tables were now turned: she was after him while he worked at keeping his distance. It was at this point that she came to me again, deeply hurt, wanting to find out what she was doing wrong.

Janice's mistake was in not allowing herself this creative period where reciprocity of interest is acknowledged but a respectful 'learning period' maintained. Premature foreclosure, letting her artist's heart have free rein, prevented her from learning some very basic things about her pursuer, even though at the beginning of his pursuit she had handled him very well and with good results. As she had mentioned earlier in her therapy, she believed that if she ever tried to control her feelings that her art would be adversely affected. This is one version of the romantic myth about feelings which many of us hold onto, and which yields similar painful results for many.

The myth

The basic myth is that we are not in control of our feelings and, following from this, that we are not responsible for them. The romantic myth is a subset of this basic myth; here we believe that we are not in charge of falling in love, that it is just something that happens to us or seizes us. In fact, the ability to choose **not** to fall in love with just anyone is necessary to life, to sanity and, especially, to a healthy and sound married life. As souls, it is true that we yearn to love – not just love our Creator – but to love all of creation, especially that highest manifestation of our creation that is our fellow human beings. As Jesus has said when asked which commandment is first: '. . . and you shall love the Lord your God with all your heart, and with all your soul, and with all your mind, and with all your strength.' Then, 'You shall love your neighbour as yourself.' He cited these commandments together then said 'There is no commandment greater than these.' But let us not confuse this expression of spiritual oneness with romance. To feel love for another, it is not necessary to fall in love. Let me clarify this by using an important aspect of my work as an example.

If, as a therapist, I did not have the capacity to love those who come to me for help, my work would not be nearly as effective. Feeling love for my clients is for me a necessary starting point and one which, fortunately, I do not have to manufacture. And the more I come to know a client, the more love I am likely to feel. The therapeutic relationship is very special in this sense. But if I permitted myself to fall in love, to cross the sometimes fine line between a caregiver and a 'lover', my work would be completely compromised, as would other aspects of my life – not least my marriage! In this case it should be utterly clear that falling in love, despite the closeness and intimate sharing that takes place in therapy sessions, would be totally unprofessional, immoral and, in most places, against the law. If therapists can and must make this choice, which is one of the stipulations of psychologists' associations worldwide, then it must be clear that falling in love is a choice that we can make. Feelings are not compromised when we do this, rather, we are exercising our power of choice. We must all simply learn to reserve our most intimate feelings for their appropriate object: our spouse.

This, then, should clarify the mental framework within which a couple embark on the task of courtship. Courtship starts with an agreement between the two that they will take some time out of their lives to get to know each other better. Hopefully, as explained in Chapter 6, some time will have been spent observing the other in various group settings. It is quite possible that the couple may already even be friends, whether long term or short term. With the intention put forward by the man, in some form or other, that he would like to court, the stakes have definitely been raised. But let us be clear as to what is being agreed to at this point and what the couple ought to be attempting to do. This is not an agreement to fall in love; rather, what the couple really want to do is to get to know each other better. A selection process has definitely already taken place, the stakes we have already said are higher, the anticipation certainly greater but, as far as possible, a certain amount of reserve and vigilance must be maintained. It should also be noted that, if this agreement to get to know each other does not lead to feelings of love or a desire to marry, it should not be viewed as a failure. Let me explain in more behavioural terms how this attitude can take shape.

Some guidelines for courtship

Throughout the courting period it is good for both the man and woman to maintain their respective home bases and independence. Nor is it necessary that the whole world even know you are courting. For many reasons, it can be a good idea to be very discreet. If, however, you have family or friends who are good confidants, this is probably a good time to call on them, to share your thoughts, impressions and experiences. Here, again, it is probably preferable for the confidants to be happily married people with proven experience, people who have a spiritual orientation and who know what it takes to build a marriage and rear a family. Such confidants as these can offer wisdom and help to keep you on a healthy path; they can help you to keep your perspective and maintain your personal boundaries, because keeping perspective and maintaining boundaries are the aspects of your will which are going to be most tested during this period. Though you may yearn to spend a lot of time with each other, at this stage it might help more to measure carefully time spent together. It is very important to maintain one's personal boundary at this point and to respect the other's.

While talking about maintaining personal boundaries, it is necessary to talk about physical contact. Our physical gestures – how we use our bodies and what contact is made with the other during courtship – are highly symbolic and indicative of inner processes and attitudes. Touches, hugs, eye contact, holding hands, caresses, kisses – all of these are highly significant and require great care and consciousness. The significance of physical gestures depends on the situation and, also, upon what one is thinking when engaging in them. A touch, for example, can be a sign that you are empathizing with the other, but if you are thinking about sex while touching it becomes, in itself, a kind of sexual activity. Physical gestures and body language can be very helpful in communication but let us be awake to what we are doing and not use this medium in a manipulative way.

We can invade another's personal space with inappropriate physical gestures, but we can also do this with words. It is one thing to say 'You are beautiful', quite another to say 'You look sexy', or 'You turn me on'. We want, at this stage, to use our physical selves and our language to further the process of getting to know one another's character while maintaining a certain crucial distance, objectivity, and respect for each other's boundaries.

In order to get to know the other better at the early stages of courtship, simple conversational formats are not enough. It is preferable to do things together and observe each other in action. For example, if the woman lets the man know that she really likes to receive flowers, then the man, in the interest of pleasing the woman, may buy her flowers on every possible occasion. It may be more profitable for the woman to see if the man – at this stage – has done this of his own accord. A couple in the romantic mode can adapt and change their behaviour quite remarkably, but seeing such changes at this time does not necessarily tell us anything about what the other person will be like as a marriage partner, or even how much they may be willing to adopt new behaviours once they are married.

I have mentioned earlier that it is quite probable that the man and woman are already friends. Along with this, it will often be true that they share many friends in common. If this is not the case, probably a good early step to take is to enter into each other's social circle. The kind of company a person keeps and the kind of relationship he or she has with friends say a lot about who they are. The other person may be all too ready to adapt his or her behaviour to your tastes, making it hard to get to know the real character, but friends are not likely to do this. If you have trouble feeling comfortable with your prospective mate's circle of friends, you will likely eventually have trouble with your prospective mate.

The best way to get to know a person is to see them in a particular situation, dealing with a certain challenge, or under stress. All this will give a clearer image than asking and answering questions. A simple example can illustrate this: She asks him at a nice dinner about his emotional attitudes, 'When you become stressed, are you clear-headed or confused?' He may give an answer that may be correct or not, but nothing can give her a better judgement than seeing him in an actual stress situation. Seeking stress situations can be of great advantage in the process of getting to know the other person. We will discuss a few examples below, all of which are meant to take place before falling in love.

Things to do

· · · · · · · · · ·

One half of the world cannot understand the pleasures of the other.

Jane Austen

· · · · · · · · · ·

1.   Go to movies, theatre, and concerts

This is perhaps a classic example, and most probably something that all single people do anyway during courtship. But in the interest of getting to know the other better, it is important to discuss what you have seen and heard in some depth. Discovering what the other person's opinion is about a certain film, the theme and the message involved, can give many clues to their mindset, attitude and general way of thinking. The choice of movie or performance of itself tells a lot about a person's interests. Someone who only likes to watch action movies definitely looks at the world in a different way from someone who only watches art movies.

2. Go shopping together

One issue, which statistically is one of the five major causes of divorce, is the handling of finances. This includes spending attitudes, which are something one usually develops while growing up. We may be lavish spenders or we may be stingy. If the attitude of each party is extremely different, it is bound to become a source of serious conflict in the marriage. A good way to find out objectively about the other person's spending attitudes is to go shopping together. One can easily tell then if the person spends a lot without calculating, or is economical, or saving, or greedy, or stingy. If one disregards this one can get into big trouble in marriage. Spending habits and attitudes towards money are very difficult to change in a person. Even if one wants to change it is a very difficult challenge. So if spending patterns are diametrically opposed, one should think twice about getting married. Attitudes towards tipping at restaurants and elsewhere can give some indication as to the generosity factor of that person. And in general, shopping can tell a lot about the person's tastes, whether it is shopping for clothes, food, electronic or household goods. One can easily get to know about the likes and dislikes of the other.

3. Cook together

Cooking is great fun for some, a pain for others. One often hears that a girl who can cook well has an advantage in being considered for marriage. Some may find it pretty old-fashioned that this should be an issue, since cooking can be learnt. There will be no attempt here to judge any view on this subject, but rather I want to explore how cooking together can be helpful in getting to know each other. There are examples where the wife hates cooking and where this has become a source of conflict in the marriage because there were unexplored expectations prior to the marriage. For those who find food important, it would be good to take the following points into consideration.

The cooking skills of a woman can say something about how in future, as a mother, she will provide a healthy diet for the children. It may also be an indication of her sense of hospitality, particularly in the eastern part of the globe where one doesn't usually invite people over to one's home without offering food. The chances that someone who hates cooking and everything around it will have an open door in their house is a bit slim. At least, in the East this will probably be the case – there may be exceptions of course.

On the other hand, there are plenty of women who would love to have a husband who can cook well and be able to run the household the same way. This is a legitimate wish, especially in a time where equality between men and women plays an ever-increasing role in society. I would recommend that all men learn how to cook at least a few types of dishes before ever getting married, as this can greatly enhance their worth as husbands and fathers.

One can easily organize a cooking event together. It brings out the skills, reveals each other's tastes, highlights difficulties in working together and, above all, it can be lots of fun.

4.   Go to the zoo together

· · · · · · · · · ·

Somethin' tells me it's all happening at the zoo.

Paul Simon

· · · · · · · · · ·

An unconventional method of getting to know another person is through his or her interaction with animals. The zoo can be an ideal setting to find out about the other person's attitude towards different animals – sensitivity, meekness, care, fears, love, and so on. Our reactions to animals often help us release emotions, and emotions which are expressed can say a lot about our character. Some people may be totally turned off by animals, while others cannot imagine being surrounded by them. Again here, extreme attitudes can cause certain unwanted challenges in marriage.

5.   Dine out

• • • • • • • • • •

*People are going on dates now to coffee bars. This is
the worst idea.
Four cappuccinos later, your date doesn't look any better.*

Margot Black

• • • • • • • • • •

A subtle way of finding out if the person is aware of formal etiquette and manners is to go out dining to a fine restaurant together. If this is an important issue for either of the two parties, then such an outing could reveal a lot. Certain movies like *Pretty Woman* and *Kate and Leopold* have tackled this issue very well. Being dressed appropriately for a particular occasion, the way one stands, sits, or orders food – all this can be found out to a certain extent at such an event. In fact, one's dress sense is an unspoken matter that plays a notable role for those who give importance to it. Being appropriately dressed for a garden party, camping, concert, seminar, work, wedding, formal or informal meeting, may be very important for many. It can become a difficult hurdle if one's expectation is great but the other person has never considered this of any importance at all. The searcher must weigh what is more important for his or herself, and decide accordingly. However, going along with the other person as she or he is, but with an inner conviction that the other can be changed in the course of time, is a dangerous way of thinking that would put a marriage at risk.

6. Drive together

• • • • • • • • • •

Natives who beat drums to drive off evil
spirits are objects of scorn
to smart Americans
who blow horns to break up traffic jams.

Mary Ellen Kelly

• • • • • • • • • •

Taking the opportunity to go for a ride in a car with the other person can also help. This may sound strange, but there is a subtle issue behind it. The way people drive through the city can give an indication of their behaviour when they are not behind the wheel. Questions that may come to the surface include: Does he or she constantly speed? Does he or she obey the traffic laws? How considerate is he or she in giving way to others in busy traffic? Is he or she impatient at rush hour (stress situation)? Does he or she use bad language in a traffic jam? Obeying traffic laws may say a lot about a person's attitude towards law and rules in general. Coping skills in stressful situations can be readily observed. Behaviour may surface which totally turns one off. In general one finds out, at least, if the person is a safe or careless driver or prone to taking risks!

7. Go to a sports event together

A sports event is a good opportunity to observe and get to know the person's emotional side. Whether it's a football game watched live in a stadium, or a baseball match – whatever it is, it can bring out anger, joy or disappointment. A whole range of feelings may come to the surface. A crowd is an environment where mass hysteria or euphoria or any kind of fanaticism can easily be aroused. The person's attitudes, restraints or any other emotional expressions will be exposed. Obviously, both of you should have some kind of interest in the sports event you attend.

8. Practise sports together

For many, being active and healthy is of huge importance. It is easy to say that one is athletic or likes to be active but the proof is in the pudding. Go out and really find out how much interest there is in a good workout or game of tennis.

9. Visit an orphanage or old people's home together

An orphanage or old folk's home may seem an unlikely venue for a date, but visits to such social institutions can be of benefit to a couple in their quest to get to know each other. One can feel uncomfortable or pity or even apathy while visiting these places, and all these possible responses (and others) reveal something about one's character and values. In fact, reactions during such visits can help to give an indication of the person's relations with their own family (e.g. respect towards the elderly, care for the helpless, etc.).

10. Visit a museum or gallery together

You may find this activity very useful in getting to know the interest or knowledge of the other person in arts. In general, such visits help to bring out many characteristics other than art, induced by the visit itself. Give it a try if you have any aesthetic sensibilities at all, and you are bound to learn something significant about the other.

11. Travel together

When the courtship period is in a more advanced stage, one of the most effective ways of getting to know the other person is to travel together. Such trips can be, of course, within one's own country or region, but it is even more effective to travel in another country with a different language and culture. Without the protective armour of one's own native tongue or the familiar trappings of one's own culture, a wide range of hidden traits can be brought to the surface. Travelling together can be revealing like nothing else and provide rare opportunities to get to know one's eventual future partner. Usually some stressful situations will arise, which can be more intense if you choose to visit a poor country or take the risk of going on an adventurous trip. Questions that arise are: How does he or she respond to, or interact with, another culture and language? Does he or she harbour prejudice towards other nations, or toward ethnic, religious, or racial groups? How does he or she cope with unhygienic situations? The list of questions here can be almost endless.

12. Serve together

Performing acts of service together is a noble and rewarding activity which brings out many latent qualities. Youth are lucky to have so many service opportunities at hand within their national or international community. However, service can be performed in many ways, and perhaps by talking about and consulting upon which service to join in the couple will learn a lot about each other. Do they care for the environment? Do they really like to help people? Do they feel good being part of a project? Are they 'giving' people or is finding their own space too much of a priority? If you are service oriented and your partner is not, there may well be clashes about how to spend your time together when you get married.

13. Visit the other person's family

• • • • • • • • • •

*Marry a woman from the mountain, and you
marry the mountain.*

Irish proverb

• • • • • • • • • •

If most of the above activities or any other activities work satisfactorily, then the final important step of visiting the other person's family needs to be included. This matter is so important that Chapter 12 is entirely dedicated to it. The above proverb puts into a nutshell why meeting and getting to know the other's family of origin is so important in the process of getting to know the other person. In meeting the other's family, much of what your potential future spouse is and will be can be unveiled before your eyes.

Becoming close

We have discussed the need to clarify and maintain boundaries during courtship. We have also looked at some of the kinds of things you can do together to get to know one another. But if your partner is passing all significant tests and you **really** want to get closer, what is the best approach?

The easiest way to feel close to another is to cross the physical boundaries and move into hugging, kissing and other physical expressions of love. But these are actually forms of nascent sexual intercourse and this is premature at this point. How and why this is will be discussed at some length in the chapter on sex and love. For now, it is enough to say that these are ways of sealing feelings of love without really knowing if true love exists between you. It is almost certain that as soon as you move into physical expressions of love, you will **feel** love and love will be a foregone conclusion. But you have much more to learn about each other first.

The more difficult approach to becoming closer to one another is to talk. Of course, you will already have talked with each other about all kinds of things, but talking as a way of achieving closeness is something different. Here, you let down your psychological guard and open up. The essence of achieving closeness verbally is in acknowledging your vulnerabilities. This means stopping the performance, getting really honest about yourself, letting go of your public self, and revealing your private self. There is, especially, a need for men to put themselves forward in this way.

· · · · · · · · · ·

It is in our faults and failings, not in our virtues,
that we touch one another, and find sympathy . . .
It is in our follies that we are one.

Jerome K. Jerome

· · · · · · · · · ·

The other side of this is listening. Here again, you have already been listening to each other, but the kind of listening that brings closeness and true understanding involves something more. In active listening you respond to the other, but the nature of your response invites further disclosure and gives assurance that you are accepting what is being revealed, warts and all.

Both of these aspects are challenging, but there is no replacement for this kind of communication. If, as a couple, this kind of verbal intimacy can't be achieved, the likelihood of achieving success in marriage is slim. However, if you are failing to get close through verbal communication and you are still sold on each other's qualities, you can seek help from a psychologist. The willingness to reach out and get help in something you are weak in is sign of maturity. Married couples often need to do this and, if they don't get help – or if they leave it too late – their marriage can be lost.

Sham intimacy

• • • • • • • • • •

Being in therapy is great. I spend an hour just talking about
myself.
It's kinda like being the guy on a date.

Anonymous

• • • • • • • • • •

Some people think they are communicating when they are really
just talking. Talking can be chatting, gossiping, backbiting,
discussing interesting subjects, or talking about your surface life.
Some of these are positively destructive (backbiting), some are a
waste of time, some are entertaining, some are useful, but none of
them are really getting to know one another on a deep and
significant level.

Many people think they are achieving intimacy when they
really are not. When I hear someone say 'He says exactly what is
on my mind,' or 'She likes all the things that I like,' or 'We are
perfect together,' I actually fear for the speaker. These statements
usually indicate that guards have been let down, that the couple are
jumping in emotionally without really getting to know each other
in a significant way. In other words, romance has taken over. The
real learning is yet to come; both of them may be surprised at the
true character of the other, and neither may be willing to live with
the faults they see. People are not perfect, and relationships are not
perfect, and making them work takes knowledge and effort.

If after all is said and done a couple do not achieve verbal
intimacy, I would say forget about going further with this relationship. Verbal communication is that important! I would go further
and say that, if you find that intimate conversation is difficult for
you, get some help before pursuing other relationships. This is a
capacity one needs to develop, especially for marriage.

✴✴✴   ✴✴✴   ✴✴✴

The important theme of courtship cannot be exhausted in one short chapter. However, we are all so different that many readers will have probably found much that they are at odds with in this chapter. It is not my intention to offer a recipe book for the highly idiosyncratic modes we will all choose in getting to know our potential future partner. There is also no question that you can ignore most of what has been said here and still 'luck out' and find yourself married to a wonderful partner. The converse is probably also true. But it is a fact that not many have 'lucked out', and there is a lot that we can all learn if we are willing to consider new ideas and new ways of doing things.

So far, I have strongly suggested the need to put off falling in love as long as possible in order to get a clearer idea of what your potential partner is really like. But the time will come in spending time together with someone whose character you admire, whose faults have been revealed, with whom honesty and openness have been achieved, that you are going to want to let your defences down and fall into that blissful state of romance about which so many yarns have been woven, so many songs sung, so much passion played out. But before you do, let's take a look at this magnificent and powerful phenomenon and see what our minds can make of it.

9

Falling in Love

. . . .

Love is the free exercise of choice.

M. Scott Peck

. . . .

This is not a 'how to', but more of a 'what is' chapter. The reason for this is that falling in love is a very easy thing to do. Given the right circumstances, the great majority of us accomplish it naturally. The basic requirement for the 'right circumstance' is essentially availability. First of all, there needs to be an available 'other'; next there needs to be an availability of mindset – to be willing to have a relationship with the available other. The simplest scenario, where there exists just one man and one woman, would probably end in them falling in love!

Real-life scenarios are not that simple. The fact of many 'others' complicates the process. Theoretically, since there are more 'others' available the possibility of falling in love should increase, but the presence of more than one other compels choosing and this factor conspires against availability of mindset. While we are deciding, we are holding back from falling in love. The very imagery of the phrase 'falling in love' suggests – quite correctly –

that it is a process of letting go. But letting go of what? Basically the answer is: letting go of restraint. Holding on, the process of restraining ourselves, takes energy and entails complexity. It is in this sense that we can say that falling in love is actually easy. It is as though we are poised at the top of a snowy slope, sitting on a sleigh with our heels dug in. All we have to do is lift our feet and we will slide down the hill. And what a thrilling ride lies ahead!

To take the metaphor of the slope and the sleigh further, we might also recognize that there are risks involved in letting ourselves go. This realization also adds to the complexity of the scenario and conspires further against availability in our mindset. To some, the fear of getting hurt becomes an almost insurmountable restraint.

The slope metaphor further applies when we consider that, once we let ourselves go down the slope, there is no looking back. Reason is no longer in play once we are going headlong down the snowy slope – we are enjoying ourselves too much and desire only to be able to stay on the sleigh. To go against the momentum of the ride would seem senseless at this point, a waste of a good slope.

The metaphor remains relevant when we come to realize that the ride will not last forever. The slope itself has an end. There comes a point in every romance when it no longer just goes by itself. Our rational faculties and our egos come into play. We have to use our own energy again and, if we want any more thrills, we have to climb up a steep slope together – and carry the sleigh to boot.

In fact, the climb back up the slope is much more analogous to the essence of marriage. It takes co-operation, energy, mutual respect, selflessness, politeness and many other capacities. If we have these capacities and use them, the climb up can also be very enriching and pleasant. Even if we lack character, the climb can help us to build it. Whether we enjoy the process of the climb or not depends largely on us. But before we ride this sleigh analogy too far (if we haven't already) let us remember simply that the ride down the hill is the easiest part. With this in mind we can return to the top of the hill and take another, more sober, look at what falling in love actually is.

Falling in love – or romantic love – is neither the beginning nor the end of love. It is one kind of love, probably the most intense. Psychologists' opinions about the value of romantic love vary greatly. Probably the majority of therapists, certainly marriage therapists, see romantic love rather negatively. We might ask why such informed, intelligent people so often see such a beautiful experience in such a negative light. The main reason is that therapists see many people who are suffering in their relationships, or suffering from their relationship. Therapists recognize that most of these relationships began with passionate romance, with the lovers saying some variation of 'He (or 'She') is everything I've ever wanted'. Just as typically, these same relationships end with feelings of extreme antipathy with the now estranged lovers saying something like 'Whatever made me marry that dolt!' It is hard to reconcile these extreme differences between these two ends of an intimate relationship. Those involved in the failed relationship often attempt to rationalize the failure by denying the affection and excitement that existed in the beginning, or by denying that the feelings were 'real'. Amnesia suddenly becomes very useful. But therapists see this and this leads many to conclude that romantic love is some kind of deception, or even sickness.

The American therapist Nathaniel Brandon is a great champion of romantic love. He regards it as one of highest, most profound achievements of human beings. This is, in fact, how most people **feel** when they are in the throes of romantic love. Brandon's description of the nature of romantic love is very good, but he admits that even the best-intentioned couples cannot keep up the intensity of romantic love for more than about seven years. After this time, Brandon's view is that the lovers should move on and find somebody else to fall in love with. He believes that we can only really be romantically involved with one person at a time but advocates serial monogamy, i.e., a string of monogamous relationships over the period of one's life. If one reads carefully, it becomes clear that there is not really much room for children in Brandon's ideas about romance.

The idea of taking romantic rides with a series of partners over one's life sounds like fun. Since so many intimate relationships fail anyway, why not legitimize this process of serial monogamy, as Brandon suggests, and just enjoy the rides while they last? We shall explore why this enticing idea is actually a dangerous proposal after we have more thoroughly examined what love – as distinct from romantic love – really is. But first, let's continue our exploration of romantic love.

A quite contrasting view of romantic love is offered by Jungian psychologist Robert Johnson. In his book *We*, Johnson retells the ancient tale of Tristan and Iseult and shows how it is a symbolic rendering of the psychological dynamics of romantic love. He explains that romantic love emerged, historically, when Christian religious sentiments were in steep decline. Many of us assume that romantic love has always existed, but this is not true. What is perhaps more surprising in Johnson's account is that romantic love emerged as a kind of secular expression of religious love. The state of ecstasy, of personal transformation, the courage, the willingness to sacrifice, the feelings of certitude which surface in romantic love are very much akin to religious experience. According to Johnson, these symptoms are appropriate in a religious experience because at these times we feel closest to divinity.

The problem with romantic love, according to Johnson, is that when we apply the sense of perfection, which is the yearning of our soul, to a mere human being, it does not really fit. When entranced lovers look into one another's eyes, according to Johnson, they are not really looking at the person, but seeing a reflection of their own soul's yearning. In this view, romantic love represents some kind of misplaced spiritual longing which when projected onto a human being ends in tragedy, as does the tale of Tristan and Iseult and other archetypal tales of love.

These few paragraphs do not do justice to Johnson's fascinating insights. His interpretation goes a long way in explaining the difficulties we are having with intimate relationships. It also helps to explain why romantic love has become such a fetish in our age which longs for spiritual fulfilment but has not found a spiritually fulfilling paradigm.

Does this mean that we should actually shun romantic love? Should we somehow refuse to take part in the ecstasy of romance? For me, the answer lies in balance, in being awake to the great potential romantic love has to delude us, to recognize the demands of mature love and to strive to build our capacities in that direction. When romance comes in the context of a relationship which is founded on maturity and spirituality, then we can allow ourselves to indulge in the pleasures of romance. In fact, as a therapist, I have come to learn that when a couple's marriage has run aground, a helpful part of the process of healing the relationship is to consciously recultivate romance. But now we are ahead of the topic at hand, for we have yet to examine the nature of mature love. Understanding this is far more central to the quest of fulfilment in marriage.

· · · · · · · · · ·

Love is a gross exaggeration of the difference between
one person
and everyone else.

George Bernard Shaw

· · · · · · · · · ·

Mature love between humans recognizes the humanity of the other. The other is not God, is not perfect; and in a mature relationship we are awake to our own imperfections as well as to the flaws of the other. But the other is also a spiritual being with a soul created in the image of God. It is part of the test and covenant of marriage that souls become intimately linked, that they are destined, if we take care, to grow as humans together towards God. Here I find truth in what psychiatrist M. Scott Peck says in *The Road Less Traveled*, that the aim of true love is always spiritual growth.

Peck also asserts that love is not a feeling, that authentic love has the capacity to transcend feelings. He goes on to say: 'In a constructive marriage . . . the partners must regularly, routinely and predictably attend to each other and their relationship no matter how they feel.' Similarly, Harville Hendrix, in his book *Getting the Love You Want*, describes love as directing our energy toward the welfare of the other. He says that it is, in this sense, 'sacrificial, but what is sacrificed is not the self but preoccupation with the self'. Love, in the view of both of these writers, is very definitely linked to our will and our capacity to choose.

As was implied in our sleigh analogy, the capacity to use our will to restrain our feelings of love may be much more important than the feelings themselves. This is specifically true at the time of courtship and getting to know one another, but the **capacity** to do this is much needed during marriage. And again, attending to each other regardless of one's feelings is much more akin to the climb up the slope than the sleigh ride down. The philosopher Rollo May devoted an important book to the relationship between love and will, in which he persuasively argued that when the dimension of will is not exercised, when moral laxity with respect to love becomes systemic in a society, that society will fall. The same could be said of marriage.

To sum up, much more important than falling in love is the need to develop in ourselves the capacity for genuine love and to keep our eyes open for that capacity in a future partner. Falling in love gets in the way, both of developing this capacity in ourselves and seeing it in the other. It is best to hold falling in love at bay until one is ready for a mature commitment and until one finds another who can reciprocate – not the feelings – but the wisdom and will to love maturely. Both partners need to be ready to take the whole spiritual journey together and this means going both down and up the slopes which both marriage and life inevitably entail.

10

Sex and Society

If I had placed 'sex' in the title of this book, the chances of its being a bestseller would have been greatly multiplied. I wonder how many readers have turned to this chapter first because of its title. Sex is something that attracts the interest of most people, whether they admit it or not. But in keeping with the spirit of this book, we will want to have a conscious look at the question of sex, and this is something most of us are not inclined to do.

Because of my spiritual orientation, many of you are perhaps wondering what the Bahá'í teachings are on this subject and how they compare with teachings of other religions. Let me say at the outset that they are similar in some respects, different in others. A brief review of sexual attitudes, both religious and non-religious, is perhaps in order.

Attitudes toward sex

· · · · · · · · · ·

People talk about 'sex' as though it hopped about by itself like a frog.
Attributed to Anne Morrow Lindbergh

· · · · · · · · · ·

All the world religions have taught that sex before marriage is not morally right. Since almost every society on earth was founded on the moral ground offered by one or more of these religions, we can safely say that the teaching of chastity before marriage was almost universal. This does not mean that the teaching was universally successfully carried out; rather, this is what the majority strove for and sex outside of marriage was considered to be reprehensible at the very least. Somewhere along the line, something happened. The present generation of young people may not be aware of what happened, and even those of us who have lived through the main period of change may not have given it much thought.

The sex drive

● ● ● ● ● ● ● ● ● ●

See, the problem is that God gives men a brain and a penis,
and only enough blood to run one at a time.

Robin Williams

● ● ● ● ● ● ● ● ● ●

To repeat a basic theme from Chapter 1, humans are essentially souls. But in this earthly life our souls are closely associated with our bodies, and thus we have to grapple with an animalistic nature. Animals have no problem with sex – they mate during mating season and that's about it. Their mating practices may be quite involved, but it all works according to instinct and towards the preservation of species. On the other hand, human sexuality has become increasingly complex. All human civilizations have had problems with human sexuality, and to some extent most individuals within these societies have struggled with some aspect of sexuality in the course of their lives. Why? Why do we humans have to complicate such a fundamentally natural and pleasurable urge?

Humans and sex

My father, a surgeon and urologist,
studied sex professionally all his life.
Before he died at 82, he told me
he hadn't come to any conclusions about it at all.

Katherine Hepburn

The reason sex has become such a complex issue for the human creature is in itself quite complex. The human brain, human society, the human soul – all these have their unique workings and demands, all are incredibly complex, and all impinge on the workings of human sexuality.

Biologists and anthropologists have often pointed out the similarities in sexual behaviour between humans and animals, but in fact a huge gulf separates the two groups. Where the gulf exists is in our minds, but it is no less real because of this. Animals, like humans, may preen themselves, prowl for a partner, compete with another of the same sex and fornicate. But, for animals, we have to assume that this is about all there is to sex. For humans, this paints a very incomplete and unsatisfactory picture. In order to complete the picture we must know what is going on in the minds of the participants before, during, and after the time these behaviours manifest themselves. The human creature could be thinking about almost anything and human sexual behaviour can be motivated by a wide variety of impulses. The feelings experienced by each partner can also be quite idiosyncratic.

The human mind is stimulated by many and various things. Place a picture in front of a person: that single stimulus can evoke manifold meanings, memories and thoughts, all of which may be particular to that person and all of which are unknown to anyone save that individual unless he or she chooses to disclose them. And even without the stimulus of a picture, human imagination can conjure one up and generate as many feelings and associations as though an actual picture had been seen.

Take this huge capacity of the human mind and conjoin it with the primitive function of sex, and the complications of human sexuality can start to be imagined. A probable reason that the human mating season lasts throughout the year is this capacity of imagination and fantasy, by which we humans can sustain thoughts about sex even when our physical drives are at low ebb. Because sex, for humans, is linked to memories and feelings, many of them deep and profound, it becomes clear that it is something much more for us than it is for other creatures.

Given this backdrop of the uniqueness of sexual feelings in humans, two significant – yet very different – facets of human sexuality stand out. First, the depth of feeling which a man can develop for a woman, and vice versa, is linked to the capacity and purpose of our soul. Finding a partner with whom we can be linked sexually, emotionally, intellectually and spiritually is an important aspect of our soul's longing and our spiritual path. Secondly, separated from this profound impulse of the soul's longing, sex can become a huge distraction from our spiritual path. The complicated interaction of sexually pleasurable sensations and fantasies with the almost infinite capacity of the human brain can result in an overwhelming, even addictive, compulsion with things sexual. Both these facets of human sexuality are, moreover, linked with our social predilections and are influenced by our social milieu. For example, our minds are wired so that pleasurable sensations concerning sex can easily be linked to our memories and fantasies. These potential links can be played upon and further developed by social stimuli, such as advertising, movies and social encounters. (If you haven't noticed how the media uses this fact, **wake up!** The media not only plays upon our sexual proclivities, we become 'sexualized' in the process. This unwittingly enlarges and twists the role of sex in our thinking.) In a similar and much more positive way, if our social milieu encourages spiritual development, the more healthy longing for profundity of emotion in the context of an enduring marital relationship will be encouraged.

Thus, the human creature lives with two powerful sexual predilections. In one, our sexual urges are linked with other facets of our being, propelling us towards wholeness on our spiritual journey. The other links our sexual desires with a vast array of attractions which tend to distract us from our spiritual purpose, entwining us with the material world and often involving us in relationships which are detrimental to our emotional well-being. The great religious figures of history must have recognized this confusing mix and therefore gave us guidelines and laws to help us move towards our spiritual purpose without getting caught in the web of attractions prompted solely by our sexual desires and the confusing range of interests which are linked to them. Let us take a look now at what changed our views and attitudes towards sex.

The erosion of religious influence

The main thing that happened to our attitudes toward sex was almost invisible to us because it was a gradual change. This change was the erosion of religion and its influence on people's lives. The process happens something like this: Religion is established in the hearts and minds of people initially through the devotion and faith of the people themselves. The founding of a religion takes tremendous sacrifice. Eventually the religion becomes established in a society and becomes the foundation of that society. Laws and norms for the society proceed from religion and are established over many generations. After a time, devotion itself – certainly in its collective form – becomes a norm. Eventually, the norms of the religion are taught to all the people – some through religious institutions but also through other institutions of society such as law courts and schools. This carries forward the process of socialization which inculcates religious values.

After a time, societies build up a kind of momentum and the process of socialization moves forward almost as though it worked on its own – an almost invisible force in people's lives (although, as we saw in Chapter 1, for each single child – and the parents who are responsible for that child – the process takes considerable energy and involves no small amount of frustration). After a time the process of socialization becomes more and more divorced from the religion which was its foundation. In the earlier stages of this 'divorce' people may continue going to collective worship, but more often because of tradition and social habit than from heartfelt devotion. In time, some people start to ask themselves why they do the things they have been socialized to do. They may not see their religious practice as relevant to their lives, which in practical terms may be more bent on making money, shopping, or going on weekend outings and holidays.

Norms other than attending collective worship also come to be questioned in the same way, and if relevant meaning is not found people gradually turn away from them. Although this process takes a period of some centuries, there are sometimes points along the way that hasten it. In the Western world, for example, the developments of science and technology came into headlong conflict with the teachings of the Church. This quickened the process of people turning away from the Church and its moral teachings.

Thus, through the ages and seasons of every major religion, there is a tendency for people to question and move away from religious norms. In response to this erosion the established religious institutions take one of two approaches. Some seek to reassert the importance of the values which ruled in the early stages of the religion. These people are generally termed fundamentalists; they come to find their identity increasingly in opposition to society. The other approach is to initiate reform, to more or less flexibly adapt themselves to the new norms so that people can continue to live in the new fashion without foregoing their religious affiliations. These are the liberals or reformists. The overall tendency, in either case, is for society to move away from the norms of the religion which were once at its heart.

The erosion of sexual norms

Let us now return to our discussion of sex and look specifically at the erosion of sexual norms in particular. We have already stated that most religious morals take energy and discipline to follow and sexual morals are no exception. The sexual appetite is a natural and powerful one. Keeping our sexual drives in line with religious teachings is no easy accomplishment, and once religious authority itself is not seen as infallible the inevitable question will arise: 'Why do I have to hold myself back from this perfectly natural impulse?'

• • • • • • • • • •

My mother was as religious as she was repressed.
Her facts-of-life speech began with the phrase,
'Satan takes many forms . . .'

Dana Gould

• • • • • • • • • •

Unfortunately, the power of sexual attraction has often become a source of fear for many influential religious figures, leading them to promote monastic or celibate lifestyles. In this way it has often been taught that the only way to spiritual enlightenment is through complete and conscious denial of the sexual appetite. Historically, in many faiths, sex was portrayed as something negative or even evil, and the masses were taught to repress sexual feelings.

Freud, repression, and sexual freedom

Sigmund Freud recognized unhealthy sexual repression in so many of his patients that the most significant aspect of his approach to psychoanalysis became geared to helping his patients overcome repression. This became the basis for much of the psychological thinking that has challenged the religious and social mores concerning sex. Together with the already declining influence of organized religion on society, this new psychological orientation brought about new attitudes, gradually encouraging many people to relax the disciplines required by their religious teachings.

An even more significant milestone was reached during the 1960s when huge numbers of young people – many of them thoughtful university students – started to challenge many of the basic mores and beliefs of their society. In the United States, for example, the country's right to go to war was challenged by young Americans, including the wider question of their country's right to draft young people into the military. Sometimes democracy was questioned. Sometimes the need to work within the system was questioned. The condemnation of drug use was reevaluated. Since alcohol was legal, why not marijuana? And, of course, what about sex? What were all the hang-ups about? In this way, many cultural and sexual mores and traditions were challenged and found wanting.

In the sexual arena, Freud's theories of repression were invoked, the challengers prevailed and the sexual revolution took hold. More particularly, Albert Kinsey's famous research, begun in the late 1940s, opened the door to a hugely liberalized attitude to all things concerning sex. This research was used as the basis of overturning laws related to sexual behaviour and is credited with providing so-called scientific evidence for a change in sexual thinking. Although much of what Kinsey and his associates 'discovered' has been discredited, the effects of their research still endure in the revised legislation of governments and in the attitudes of the sexual revolution it helped fuel.

The sexual revolution

• • • • • • • • • •

Sexual intercourse began
In nineteen sixty-three
(Which was rather late for me)
Between the end of the Chatterley ban
And the Beatles' first LP.

Philip Larkin

• • • • • • • • • •

The sexual revolution is probably the most widespread and enduring of the legacies of the 1960s and the 'hippie' era. Since then, repression has been seen as the enemy and social forces have shifted dramatically away from anything encouraging modesty. Chastity has become a word almost dropped from our vocabulary; the word 'virginity' evokes giggles and is something which, if possessed, is rarely admitted to.

• • • • • • • • • •

Mom! We had such an interesting lesson in school today.
It was all about minotaurs, dragons, elves, sphinxes, virgins,
and other mythical creatures.

Schoolchild

• • • • • • • • • •

Freedom has become the watchword in the sexual domain. Chastity, which began as a religious standard and was later adopted as a social one, is now seen as a social anachronism and is maintained as a standard only within relatively isolated and insular religious communities. Since sexual freedom has come to be the new social standard, anything that seeks to limit sexual expression has to be explained before it is legitimized. All such legitimizations are bound to be challenged if they don't include an aspect of sexual satisfaction. A post-sexual-revolution adult (starting as early as 12 years old), if not sexually satisfied, is seen as having a 'problem', someone who is not quite well socialized.

Fruits of the sexual revolution

With all the sexual freedoms afforded in these post-sexual revolution times, a huge irony has surfaced. According to the authors of *Sex in America*, the sexually most satisfied population in the United States is the married, monogamous, Evangelical Christian. This is the group with among the most conservative, traditional attitudes toward sex! This finding was probably contrary to almost everyone's expectations. But if we recognize that humans are essentially souls, we can begin to understand why sexual freedom does not often bring happiness, not even sexual happiness. The primary requisite to being more conscious about sex and sexuality is the recognition that healthy sexuality must be founded on the fact of our essentially spiritual makeup.

While the sexual revolution may have helped free us from sexual repression, it was not founded upon spiritual vision or insight. And although it was initially welcomed by many women, perhaps because it was contemporaneous with the women's movement, some leading feminists came to see the sexual revolution as antithetical to women's emancipation. The increase in single mothers is partly linked to the sexual revolution and here women (and their children) usually stand to lose most. The pain, anguish and confusion of serial relationships – so much a pattern of the post-sexual revolution society – is also partly a result of greater sexual freedom. The increase in sexually transmitted diseases and the HIV/AIDS epidemic is also linked to the sexual revolution. It is beginning to look as though the only winners in the sexual revolution are those who did not buy into it! Let's explore in more detail why this is.

Meanings of sex

The facet of our sexuality that confuses us is the pure pleasure we get from sexual sensations and the manifold directions this takes when linked to the human mind. I have said earlier that for an animal, sex is simply an appetite, and this appetite seeks appeasement only at limited times of the year. For humans, when divorced from our true purpose in life, sex can take on numerous meanings and expressions. Here are some of them:

- A way of dominating the other – both men and women have their own ways of using sex as a way of gaining power over, or manipulating, the other.

- Fleeting fun – sex is meant to be enjoyable, but not just to be used as a source of enjoyment divorced from deep human feeling and mutual belonging.

- Business – prostitution is said to be the world's oldest profession. And today's pornography business is a huge money-earner. Besides this, sex is used in advertising all kinds of products, and movies without a sex scene are not considered to be a good business risk for producers.

• • • • • • • • • •

The big difference between sex for money and sex for free is that sex for money usually costs a lot less.

Brendan Behan

• • • • • • • • • •

- Perversion – almost anyone, any animal, and any thing can become a sex object for humans. Paedophilia has become the source for cross-national trafficking in children.

• • • • • • • • • •

My schoolmates would make love to anything that moved, but I never saw any reason to limit myself.

Emo Philips

• • • • • • • • • •

- A show of strength – this is usually for males, a way of proving manhood.

- An obligation – sex can be expected as a means of showing that you love a person or that you are open as a person (i.e., not repressed).

- A habit – once our minds get on a sexual track, there is a tendency to move on that track again and again.

- An addiction – this is an extension of habit, when we feel we **have** to go down the sexual track, either physically or in our minds. Sex can be very addictive.

- An assertion of one's sexual identity – a way of showing others you are a woman or a man.

- A confirming of one's sexual identity – a way of showing **yourself** you are a woman or a man.

- Conquest – here sex is used as a form of hunting, of catching your prey. Earlier this was mainly the domain of men, but it is now used more and more by women.

- Stress relief – life is full of stress and people look everywhere for relief. Sex has a temporary stress relief chemical component.

- Revenge – sex is often used to get back at people for past real, perceived or imagined misdeeds.

- Experiment – try it out! This is an experimental age. Note: this is not experiment in the scientific sense of the word, although sex has been used for this as well.

• • • • • • • • • •

He that breaks a thing to find out what it is,
has left the path of wisdom.

J. R. R. Tolkien

• • • • • • • • • •

- Abuse – there are many ways to seriously hurt and injure people with sex.

- An expression of anger – we can be just generally angry people, or have some specific issue over which we are angry, and sex can be used to show this.

- An expression of love – sex can be used to express love for the other, potentially for many others.

- An expression of insecurity – not very many who engage in sex outside marriage are really that sure of themselves. This is usually a boundary issue.

- Rebellion – this is a variation on the revenge theme, but usually against parents or other figures of authority.

- A show of freedom – sex can be used to show we are free. Most of the time, though, we are showing our enslavement to sexual impulses.

- Attraction – sex can be used to show we are attracted to another. But the fact of a sexual attraction does not mean we should engage in sex.

. . . .

You use sex to express every emotion except love.

Woody Allen

. . . .

It's no wonder that opening the door to sexual freedom has failed to bring us happiness. After a while it becomes hard enough to be awake to what sex means to us, how much more difficult to understand what it means to our sexual partner(s). Augmenting our hurt and confusion in the sexual arena is the fact that sexual intercourse is probably the most intimate physical act – the closest two human bodies come to being one (Siamese twins excepted!).

When a couple engages in sex, if their minds are connected to their bodies a significant attachment to the other person is inevitable. Their bodies are saying, 'I am yours and you are mine.' If this couple then break up, profound, deep hurt is naturally felt. A gaping wound is left which takes time and consciousness to heal and which almost always leaves a scar, even when we give it time (which most do not). We are then less whole for our next partner and the longer our series of relationships are, the more wounded, scarred and confused we become. This is **not** happiness!

The schizoid personality

As implied by the previous paragraph, there is another route by which we can to some degree preserve ourselves from deep hurt and yet 'enjoy' sexual freedom. We do this by separating our mind from our body. This is not something most people set out to do consciously. It is a largely unconscious mechanism for survival which kicks in when sex is used in ways that run counter to our spiritual being. It protects us from feeling profound pain, humiliation, shame, defeat, and hopelessness – but results in our becoming schizoid.

• • • • • • • • • •

And as the human heart, as fashioned by God, is one and
undivided,
it behoveth thee to take heed that its affections be, also,
one and undivided.

Bahá'u'lláh

• • • • • • • • • •

The schizoid personality is one which has lost touch with its soul's longing. There are many ways by which we do this, but in the area of relationships the schizoid personality 'engages' in sex without being wholly involved. In these post-sexual revolution times, the schizoid personality has become the norm and is reflected in the 'hardness' of the workplace, the lack of satisfaction in other areas of life, the seemingly endless arrays of ways we seek relief from stress, but never really getting it because life itself is not felt as meaningful. In most ways, society has itself become schizoid. Playing with sex, using it in ways not intended for our development, has contributed to the hollowness of our age.

The irony is that in the field of relationships the schizoid personality gets its start by enjoying sexual freedom but, in time, comes not to enjoy sex as deeply as those who with consciousness and discipline choose to place the value of their spiritual development first. This is because the schizoid personality's ability to feel becomes numbed as its mind becomes less engaged. In fact, not only are sexual pleasures numbed, but all feelings become attenuated, pushing the schizoid personality to greater extremes in order to seek satisfaction. This is a never-ending, corroding and hollow pursuit (T.S. Eliot's 'The Hollow Men' is a profound exposition of the schizoid personality) which never fulfils.

· · · · · · · · · ·

Must we find a solution?
Can't we just enjoy the problem for a while?

Graffiti

· · · · · · · · · ·

❖❖❖ ❖❖❖ ❖❖❖

We are children of the sexual revolution. As a result, most of us have unwittingly bought into an orientation that is schizoid. If you have been engaging in sexual relationships without being married and totally committed to your marriage partner, then you may well resist accepting much of what has been put forward in this chapter. Or perhaps you are starting to feel guilty or blame-worthy for sexual contacts you have had or still have. It is not my intention to lay guilt trips. I was part of the sexual revolution myself and was greatly influenced by the new tide of behaviour it brought in its wake. But we have lessons to learn from this social experiment, and however painful this may be we need to re-examine our attitudes and reconsider the choices we are making. This is going to take some time.

Sexually, we have been hurting ourselves. Only through acknowledging the superficiality of our sexual pursuits and seeking healing from our schizoid patterns, can we begin to achieve wholeness. We and our society need healing in many ways and one of these ways is through sexual healing. The way we can do this will be addressed in the next chapter.

11

Sexual Healing

In the previous chapter we examined primarily the complications that ensue from using sex in ways that run counter to our soul's purpose. In this chapter we want to explore the role of sex in a spiritual context. Through doing this we will gain clarity and be in a position to heal ourselves of the ubiquitous messages which lead our minds into the maze of emotional and psychological confusion discussed in the last chapter. As we have seen, society itself has become schizoid, and since this has become our cultural matrix, effort needs to be exerted if we are to achieve clarity and health. We need to discover what sex is in terms of our spiritual purpose. This is a necessary component of preparing ourselves for marriage and finding a partner who is also prepared. Again, we will have to widen our view and look at the big picture.

Our future children

When looking for a partner, many do not consider that the reason for finding a partner is to get married. We have discussed earlier the need to be focused on this, that not doing so is a form of escape which tends to erode our capacities and lead us into confusion. Beyond this, we should also remember that one of the main purposes of marriage is to have children and to provide a safe, secure and wholesome upbringing for them. It is worthwhile meditating upon the needs of children when preparing for marriage, because this will help us to understand what children require of their parents, and thus what we need to prepare ourselves for and what to look for in a future partner.

The needs of children

· · · · · · · · · ·

*The most important thing a father can do for his children
is to love their mother.*

Theodore M. Hesburgh

· · · · · · · · · ·

The foremost principle of child-rearing is to provide a loving, secure environment. The first requirement for such an environment is the relationship between the mother and father. If the channel of affection between the parents is open, the children feel secure, even if other factors such as material means may be lacking. On the other hand, if the parents do not feel love towards one another, even if there is no blatant fighting, the children feel it. Children are like emotional sponges and pick up on everything that happens between their parents. Even if they are not conscious of what is going on, they feel when things are not right and are deeply affected. Parents are their children's lifeline, but in a way the love they feel for each other is even more important than the love they have for their child.

Purity

The sensitivity of children with respect to their parent's relationship requires a vigilance and purity which can be daunting. One factor which obviously adulterates the parental relationship and severely affects the healthy development of children is lack of fidelity. Infidelity affects the children, even if it is kept hidden. In fact, because the children are deeply affected by it, if they do not **know** about it, this lack of conscious knowledge will make dealing with the effects of their parent's infidelity even more difficult when they are adults.

Sexual infidelity is an obvious infringement upon the integrity of the marital relationship. In many societies, adultery is considered a crime and, in terms of its spiritual and emotional effects, it truly is. Interestingly, studies have shown that, even in these sexually liberal times when most do not think premarital sex is wrong, the majority of adolescents believe that sexual infidelity in marriage is not acceptable. Adolescents have parents, and they do not want their parents to have other sexual partners. In fact, children want their parents to be together, to stay together, to love each other and to be forever faithful in their love. In truth, we want this of our parents even into our adulthood.

Chastity revisited

Most people nowadays have a built-in resistance to the idea of chastity. So seldom is this concept addressed that many people have come to confuse the word chastity with celibacy, so allow me to clarify this. Celibacy is the renouncing of all sexual activity for the whole of one's life. Vows of celibacy, for example, are what Roman Catholic priests and nuns take, following the Catholic belief that living without sex and not being married somehow links them more closely with the life of Jesus because He was not married. The implication of this is that engaging in sex, even if married, makes us spiritually inferior. I want to clarify that this is **not** in any way the view taken here.

Chastity is the development of purity in one's thoughts and actions. Having sexual relations with one's marital partner does not in any way diminish one's purity. It is, in fact, a healthy expression of one's love and devotion. But what of other sexual thoughts and actions? This is where our resistance comes in. The standard of chastity has largely been discarded. We live, now, in a world, that encourages an ever more open orientation to sexual activity of all kinds under all conditions. What crosses the line of acceptability today will likely become acceptable in a few years time. We are all nurtured within this liberalizing matrix. Thus, it is natural that we have 'opened up' and are becoming ever more sexually active and stimulated. Many people reading this book will have had sexual relationships and some may already be living with their partner without being married. And those who are not may either be hiding the fact or be feeling a certain amount of shame in their relative inexperience whenever the subject of sex is raised. This is the source of our resistance to the idea of chastity.

I accept and understand whatever resistance you may have to chastity because, in the present climate, it is natural. You may not feel in any position to make changes in your living situation, your present relationship or your lifestyle. This I can also appreciate. You may already have had to 'adjust' your ideas about sex in order to be with your present partner and you may not be at all inclined to 'readjust' them now. Many of the ideas in this book about love are hard for people to accept, but the ideas about sex seem to be the most difficult. While I am critical of the incredible amount of preoccupation our society has with sex, I do **not** encourage a preoccupation with not having sex.

Purity is an aspect of our soul. When aspects of our soul are ignored, we become mentally and physically numb to them. When we open our minds to consider spiritual truths about our soul, our soul's desire for fulfilment can kick in, and we may feel a desire to nurture what has been neglected. When this happens, a process takes place that can open the door for healthy change in our lives. This is what I hope to accomplish in introducing the spiritual – and ultimately – practical concept of chastity.

One practical component of chastity has to do with our wish and intent to be a faithful partner in marriage. Chastity is not something that just happens out of the blue. Nurturing this aspect of our soul takes on different forms before and after marriage.

There is a relationship between our sexual attitudes and behaviour before marriage and after marriage.

· · · · · · · · · ·

Before marriage absolutely chaste,
after marriage absolutely faithful to one's chosen companion.

Shoghi Effendi

· · · · · · · · · ·

I have often asked women in my workshops how they would feel if their husband were to leer at another woman or to look at another woman with sexual desire. The overwhelming response is that women find this humiliating and disrespectful in the extreme. I recently heard of a young woman taking delight in the physical attractiveness of a man on a television programme she was watching with her boyfriend. Although this was a kind of playful teasing, her boyfriend got so frustrated that he got up and walked out of the room in a huff. Both sexes are offended by this kind of leering behaviour, yet in the present liberalized sexual climate most of us are likely to feel that we ought to 'overlook' it. But this kind of behaviour affects the whole family, including our own selves. Probably just having thoughts for another has similar effects. All unchaste behaviours and thoughts to some extent adulterate a marriage and affect our children.

· · · · · · · · · ·

And if he met the fairest and most comely of women,
he would not feel his heart seduced by the least shadow of
desire for her beauty.

Bahá'u'lláh

· · · · · · · · · ·

If we could see more clearly the effects an unchaste life has on us, on those close to us, and ultimately on our society, our standards and attitudes regarding chastity would be much more finely tuned and we would want to develop this virtue so that it could extend into all areas of our life. There is a connection between our sexual past and our future married life. In marriage, we need to be able to control our thoughts, eyes, and behaviour, and this capacity does not come out of nowhere. This control needs to be practised before marriage.

Sexual experience

One argument often levelled against the practice of chastity before marriage is that sex is important in marriage and so it is important to see if you and your partner are sexually compatible before you get married. In fact, it is often said that we need to learn a lot about our partners before getting married and that the best way to do this is to live together first, and in this way you can learn all you need to learn before making a commitment to marry. Of course, this argument is extended by many to question the utility of marriage in the first place. Why not just live together? If it works, fine, if it doesn't, move on to another relationship until you find someone who is compatible.

In considering these arguments, which on one level can seem quite logical, we need, again, to cultivate a wider perspective, one that takes into account the children that can result from these unions, as well as our spiritual purpose and the role of sex in light of this. We know, for example, that divorce adversely affects children. It can be argued that in some cases divorce is preferable to the kind of hell that some couples experience in marriage, but it still remains true that children are deeply hurt and carry wounds from the broken unions of their parents.

Because so many marriages end in divorce these days a lot of people are reconsidering the viability of marriage as an institution. But what of those relationships where couples choose to just live together without being married? How do they fare? In the United Kingdom, when in the early 90s the divorce rates hovered around 30 per cent, the break-up rate of couples who lived together **and** had children together was three times that amount! We don't have up-to-date figures for non-wed couples breaking up, but the divorce rate in Britain is now 42 per cent. Put this together with the fact that by 2006, for the first time the number of children born out of wedlock exceeded those born within a marriage. These are statistics we rarely hear about. Also, for those who think marriage is ultimately important but that it is good to live together first, the success of those marriages tends to be less than for those marriages which are contracted before the couple move in together.

To many, the foregoing facts seem to be counter-intuitive. Practice should make perfect. Having options should give us comfort. If we had the option to take back cars that didn't perform well or after we had accidents, we might after several purchases find a car which is truly better (and we might, in time, learn how to treat cars). But because we do not have this option, we are more likely to take a lot of care to look into the condition and reliability of cars (and how to drive and take care of them) **before** we purchase them. Perhaps marriage is something like this. If we know it involves a serious commitment and a lot of maturity from the start, we are more likely to take meaningful steps to prepare ourselves. The tendency now is to prepare less and try people out more and the result is a huge glut in the 'used partner market' with an indeterminable amount of damage done to each one!

Although sex is a significant aspect of marriage, it is much more important to know if our future partner has developed chastity than it is to know how good they are in bed. Obviously you can't learn both at once! When you start to feel love for another, it is natural to be sexually attracted. But if you can show the maturity to postpone sexual involvement until after you are married, you show the kind of character that tends to make a good marriage partner. There are times, for example, after marriage when your marriage partner may not be available or when other attractive opportunities present themselves – you need to be able to forgo sex at these times or your marriage will definitely be in jeopardy.

• • • • • • • • • •

My wife – God bless her – was in labour for thirty-two hours.
And I was faithful to her the entire time.

Jonathan Katz

• • • • • • • • • •

To develop chastity and other virtues is to develop character, and character is a foundation upon which marriage can be built. When we build a house, we build the foundation first and if it is good we can be confident the house will be a good place to live. Even if repairs need to be made and renovations are called for, the house itself will still stand and can be trusted. If marriage is analogous to building a house, sex may be analogous to putting on the roof. This goes on last, certainly after the foundation; it is helpful in keeping out the rain and definitely adds to the comfort of living in the house. It also gives a feeling of completion. But it cannot be compared to the foundation in importance, nor can it take precedence. Sex has a definite and significant place in marriage, but to engage in sex before marriage is to put the cart before the horse. Things are out of order and we can't expect them to go right.

Love and sex

• • • • • • • • • •

The modern Little Red Riding Hood,
reared on singing commercials,
has no objection to being eaten by the wolf.

Marshall McLuhan

• • • • • • • • • •

While these standards for the development of purity are at odds with present-day standards related to sex, they work very well for the development of our souls. The archetypal yearning of our souls with respect to intimate relationships is this: we want to find a partner whom we can love from now to the end of time. We want to be united emotionally, intellectually and spiritually. We want to be with this partner, to develop a life with this partner, to have and raise children with this partner, and we want to seal this covenant and express this love, union and commitment with the most intimate form of physical expression available to us. This, of course, is sex. And sex also happens to be the means by which we can have children together. It all fits! This is the context in which sex not only finds its place for humans, it serves to enhance, most wonderfully, all that we want to express in this most intimate of human unions.

Here we find the wisdom in the joining of this primeval instinct with the remarkable and complex workings of the human mind. Our minds serve to enrich and multiply the feelings and thoughts and add profound dimensions to what is otherwise just a physical release. And in the context of the marital union with our one beloved, we can experience this in depth, full of trust, free of adulteration. But this kind of freedom is not won easily, especially in today's world. It is won through the development of character, one of the conditions being chastity, requiring both discipline and faithfulness to the teachings of our Creator.

Love is not enough

I want to point out and emphasize here that love is not a sufficient condition for healthy sexual expression. Many believe that where love exists for another, it is natural and correct to express that love sexually. This is also used, usually by males but increasingly by females, to kind of blackmail or lead the other into sexual activity: 'You love me, don't you? Then why don't we do it?' or 'Why wait if the feelings are there?' The fact is that the human creature is a lot more complex than this and many other conditions need to be met before sex finds its rightful and truly healthy place. If we are going to be conscious in courtship, we need to keep conscious about the role of sex.

The scenario where chastity is perhaps put to the greatest test is when we not only feel love for our partner but are sure that we are going to stay together even if, for one reason or another, we are not actually making a formal commitment to marriage right now. Even here the ability to establish and maintain boundaries is important. The discipline this takes and the respect for the other person's boundaries it inculcates is most helpful for a couple when they do decide to actually marry. And let's be honest with ourselves: if we aren't, for any reason, choosing to marry now, how can we be sure that we will actually marry this person? Putting off sexual contact is not only a good test of character, it also engenders decisiveness and seriousness and is more likely to move a couple forward in a healthy direction.

In significant ways, although humans are much more than simply biological creatures, even our biology gives us signs as to the role of sex. Sex gives rise to procreation. Thus, biologically speaking, having sex connotes 'We will have children together'. The development of modern contraceptives may change this intellectually for us, but it does not change our archetypes, which are the most deeply embedded aspects of our psyches.

Gynaecologist Sharon Hillier has pointed out that when women engage in sex a kind of revolution takes place within their bodies. An adjustment has to be made to the bacterial environment to accommodate the 'intrusions' of the male. Once this is done the female body then recognizes the body of the male partner and no new adjustments are required. However, the intrusion of a different male body tends to throw the woman's homeostatic system off, often resulting in vaginal infections. Could this be a biological signal for monogamy?

Biologists have also found that when a couple are involved with each other sexually, hormones are secreted which tend to evoke feelings of love and union. Thus, sex can have the beneficial effect of helping a couple to stay together, even when other aspects of their relationship may be stressful or conflicted. This is a definite plus for married couples. Unfortunately, this component of sexual encounter also promotes similar feelings for a partner that you may have no plans to stay with. In other words, if you start having sexual relations with someone, you may feel that you are in love with that person and want to stay with them, even if all other signs are to the contrary. The lesson here, again, is not to have sex with someone you are not already prepared to commit yourself to.

A further and very significant benefit for couples who adhere to a standard of chastity is that, in closing the door to physical expressions of closeness, they are pushed to develop the capacity to relate to each other verbally in order to develop and sustain a bond. This is especially important for men, who tend to be weak in this area – which is one of the reasons males tend to push for sexual involvement. The kind of bond developed through verbal intimacy is much more fundamental and important than a sexual bond. If a couple are unable to develop a verbal connection with each other, they have no business getting married, but if they substitute this with a sexual connection they can fool themselves into thinking they can have an enduring and successful relationship.

• • • • • • • • • •

This wasn't conversation. This was oral death.

Edna Ferber

• • • • • • • • • •

The need for a new model of courtship

These are troubled times for relationships. Confusion abounds. A plethora of books, magazines, talk shows, movies, Internet sites, therapies – all geared to coming to terms with finding love in relationships – testify to the fact that we are in an age of transition. We are searching for something we haven't found yet, individually and socially. Sex is implicated in all of this. We have seen that the best way to find sexual fulfilment is to keep our spiritual reality in view. We need to develop our characters, including purity and discipline. Ideally, society should provide us with a model we can strive to live by, but since society itself is in a period of transition, it has no healthy model to offer. We need the courage to strike out in directions different from those taken by most people, we need to make the effort to establish a pattern in our own life which is wholesome and practicable and, in time, these workable individual patterns will take hold and society will take them on. In the meantime, we cannot expect much social reinforcement in our efforts to become conscious about sexual matters. We are pioneers, striking out new pathways, and this takes courage and faith.

• • • • • • • • • •

Most people are more comfortable with old problems
than with new solutions.

Anonymous

• • • • • • • • • •

When a child is young, its parents may be stern about not playing with fire. The child is made to obey. When the child grows into adolescence, it does not simply obey, it wants to see what playing with fire is all about. In the process it gets burned or causes mishaps and, eventually, learns the wisdom about how to handle fire. Growing up sexually is something like this. We are collectively at a stage where our experimentation with sexual freedom has got us into trouble, personally and socially, and it is time to arrive at a conscious understanding of sexuality in our personal lives and gradually work for its implementation into a new social paradigm.

We have come out of our collective childhood where we lived in a kind of blind obedience to religious and social authority, where people were taught to fear sex and repress it all costs. We now need to come out of our collective adolescence, where we are reacting to our authoritarian past and experimenting with new ways of being sexual. In doing this, we are pioneering the coming of age of a conscious sexuality, where we recognize but control our sexual urges for a higher purpose.

Developing our souls

· · · · · · · · · ·

To be pure and holy in all things
... is a necessary characteristic
of the unenslaved mind.

'Abdu'l-Bahá

· · · · · · · · · ·

I hope the preceding sections have given some idea of the role of sex in a spiritual and healthy relationship and the challenges this presents in the present social context. Later on, I will give an overview of what I consider to be viable models that could be taken on by our society as more of us mature in the way we pursue courtship. Sex for humans is a complicated matter and we need to be awake to our sexuality and conscious about how and when we express it. Developing chastity will probably always be a challenge, especially for young single people. But in these times when sexual messages are used to promote all kinds of products and sell movies, music, magazines, books and all kinds of other things, and given that the bells of the sexual revolution are still ringing, it is especially challenging.

Should we be angry that this society has become so pre-occupied with sex? Should we be upset that our parents and schools and other social institutions are not providing us with healthy models of courtship and supporting healthy attitudes to sexual behaviour? Well, these are just a few among the huge number of seeming injustices in our world, and we need to start from wherever we are. In this we have no choice. This is a challenge to our spirit; if we rise to it, we will grow and develop and reap dividends both spiritually and materially.

The fetish that our present-day societies have with things sexual is a symptom of our enslavement. It is a mindless trap. Waking up to this reality will enable us to win the kind of liberty that is true and enduring. Recovery from our present-day schizoid condition will give us a freedom which is soul-felt and cannot be taken away. The choice is ours.

• • • • • • • • • •

Arise, O people,
and, by the power of God's might,
resolve to gain the victory over your own selves,
that haply the whole earth may be freed and sanctified
from its servitude to the gods of its idle fancies –
gods that have inflicted such loss upon, and are responsible for
the misery of their wretched worshippers.

Bahá'u'lláh

• • • • • • • • • •

12

Parents

• • • • • • • • • •

*The reason grandparents and grandchildren get along so well
is that they have a common enemy.*

Sam Levenson

• • • • • • • • • •

M arriage is a rite of passage. It is one of those significant
crossroads in life when you inevitably go through a
transition, when you say goodbye to part of who you were and
take on an expanded identity. Parents, other family members, and
friends come to a wedding to witness and take part, because they
too are part of this rite of passage. Their lives in relation to the
couple will be changed. The couple themselves will be setting up
their own home. They will begin the process of establishing their
own unique family culture, distinct from that of their parents.
They will not be 'single' people any more, but everyone will be
relating to them as a couple. In a healthy societal setting, the
wedding signals the fact that neither are 'available' any more for
overtures of courtship.

There has been a tendency in the modern world to blur these
turning points, perhaps to make them seem more manageable or

to keep from facing the fear which quite naturally accompanies these transitions. The fact that many couples choose to live together before getting married is an example of this. When the wedding comes, everyone still plays their part: if it is a religious ceremony, the religious authority still convenes, the parents and other family members come, the friends are there, the presents are given, the seeing of the couple off on their new life – but somehow their new life has already started and there is a certain hollowness to the whole affair. When the couple leaves for their honeymoon they have already consummated their marriage months, perhaps even years, before. They are going back to a home they have already established – all they need to do is find a place for the wedding presents.

To me, this all-too-common modern-day wedding is out of focus. Everyone's role is somehow blunted and the rite anti-climactic. It is all indicative of the failing strength of marriage itself. Instead of hope for the newlyweds' success in their future life, the question in so many people's minds is 'How long is it going to last?' This points to the couple's lack of preparation and consciousness in the courtship process. It also highlights the 'me' orientation and lack of connection to family and to the world of which they are a part. In giving precedence to their own desires, they deprive themselves of valuable input from others, especially their parents.

Unconsciously, couples are by-passing crucial human archetypes such as Mother, Father, Maiden and Suitor, Bride and Groom. Let's take a step back for a moment, and look at the experience of a couple's coming together from the perspective of their parents. In this we will see the significant role that parents play in the process, from beginning to end, and how important it is that they feel a part of something of which they are, in fact, undeniably a part. We will need, also, to clarify where the boundaries lie, and how they change when a couple gets married. I am also writing this chapter for parents, so that in reading it they can perhaps gain additional insight into the importance of their role at this time.

The Mother and Father archetypes

Mother and Father are perhaps the most deeply embedded of all human archetypes. We all have a mother and a father, although in some cases we may not know who they are. Even in cases of orphans or children who have been adopted, the spectre of their mother and father – even if they never knew them – stays with them throughout their lives. There may well be anger over the fact that their parents have left them and sometimes this anger translates itself into 'I don't care about them', but in fact our natural parents – who represent the archetype – always have an important place in our psyche. They conceived us, our mother bore us, and even if they are absent from our lives, we will always wonder about them and about their love – or, on the shadow side, their lack of love – for us.

The trials of parenthood

In the more usual cases, our natural parents raise us. If not, then there always must be substitute caregivers towards whom the role of parents is transferred. As we saw in Chapter 1, human babies are absolutely dependent upon their caregivers and take a huge amount of attention and energy for a much longer time than for other creatures. It takes responsibility and maturity to raise children, often far more than parents are ready for. Most parents grow into being parents and learn lessons about parenting along the way. This process is usually not very smooth. Some parents feel overwhelmed by the requirements of being caregivers and providers. The relationship between them at this time is often taxed to the limit or, all too often, reaches breaking point.

In almost all cases, parents are doing all they can with the resources they have. Even in cases of abuse, the parent feels some kind of maternal or paternal love for the child, but they themselves may not have received the nurturing they needed and, in the pressure cooker of what Carl Whitaker calls the family crucible, are not able to find appropriate ways of juggling their own felt needs with the never-ending needs of their children and spouse.

Most parents ache to give all they can to their children, but doing this while having also to meet the material demands – or felt demands – of the family is often extremely taxing. Many parents want for their children what they themselves have never had. Some parents want their children to achieve what they never achieved. Some parents live almost wholly for their children and almost all parents have had to sacrifice for the sake of raising them. I am not saying that the degree of sacrifice is always wise or entirely selfless. Sometimes parents' desires for their children are driven by their own unmet needs in their marriage or in their upbringing.

The special bonds between parent and child

The bond between parent and child is always significant. We are not really aware of what our caregivers were going through as parents while we were still children. Our earliest years are completely out of our memory; even the memories we do have of our later childhood years are coloured by our undeveloped child's mind. While we are children our parents loom large, they are almost god-like figures. We are not aware of the insecurities they felt or the fears they may have had.

The imprints of our parents within us

• • • • • • • • • •

Every marriage is a battle between two families struggling to reproduce themselves.

Carl Whitaker

• • • • • • • • • •

I have said earlier that children are like sponges, that they feel what is happening with their parents, for example when there is a conflict. I want to clarify, however, that children do not

understand what is happening. Usually, in fact, when there are problems between mother and father, the child sees itself as somehow the source of the problem. Sometimes a child **becomes** a problem because of what is happening between its parents. When one or both of the parents are upset with the child, the child is more likely to take a stance of defending itself, but even here, children do not see clearly what is really happening and can only begin to truly understand it if they develop insight as adults.

Our parents are with us all the time, even when they are not physically present. Parents face real responsibility when they have children. In many ways they rise to the challenge and show character, and these strengths can be taken on by their children. In other ways, they – and the relationship between them – are found wanting. Their children swallow but do not digest all of this. We internalize the strengths and weaknesses of our parents and other significant caregivers, without knowing what it is we are ingesting. The bewildering maze and knots of our families are introjected, becoming part of our shadow self. In this way we become a mystery to ourselves which can only be potentially unravelled when we ourselves face the challenges of marriage and being parents.

· · · · · · · · · ·

I grew up to have my father's looks,
my father's speech patterns,
my father's opinions,
and my mother's contempt for my father.

Jules Feiffer

· · · · · · · · · ·

The challenge adolescence brings

The interface between the period when we internalize the ways of our parents and the period where we ourselves take on adult responsibilities is known as adolescence. Adolescence, as we have already discussed, is a period of transition. Traditional societies

. . . .

The invention of the teenager was a mistake.
Once you identify a period of life in which people
get to stay out late
but don't have to pay taxes –
naturally, nobody wants to live any other way.

Judith Martin

. . . .

have rites of passage for adolescents who have come of age, but our modern world has no clear indicator for adulthood and no single rite through which a young person passes to know that he or she has come of age. Adolescence begins with puberty, which for modern children begins generally earlier than in previous times. But the length of the adolescent period has been extended even further in the other direction. Since there is no clear rite of passage it is, of course, difficult to ascertain when adolescence ends, but the psychological realization of adulthood is something that comes very late for many people. Being over thirty is no guarantee that we have grown up. In many pre-modern societies, being over thirty was considered old age!

Society itself is, as we have seen earlier, in a period of transition which, interestingly enough, is characterized in the Bahá'í writings as coming of age. As I have pointed out in the introduction to this book, we seem to be working hard to delay our collective arrival at maturity. We have not come to terms with growing up. When we do grow up collectively we will, in all probability, be able to delineate adolescence more clearly and move through it more decisively.

For parents, the period when their children move into adolescence can be extremely taxing. As we clarified in Chapter 1, becoming fully human is a complex and trying process. The socialization which takes place involves pain, and much of what occurs happens on an unconscious level, both for the child and the parents. For the child, there are felt injustices, confusion about what it is all about, and anger over all the curtailment of natural instincts and desires which growing up seems to entail. When the child moves into adolescence there are physiological factors of puberty which often cause the thinking of young adolescents to lose perspective. These are physiological changes in the brain chemistry which tend to cause befuddlement, and parents are often the ones befuddled! It helps to know that there can be physiological reasons for some of our adolescents' perplexing behaviour.

Then there are all the issues of growing up which come home to roost at this time. Often the adolescent feels that he or she is not prepared for the adult world. This, in fact, is often the case. Parents tend to be lax in spending much-needed time with their children in earlier years, talking to their children about their lives and teaching the importance of developing character. To complicate matters further, there are the fears which the adolescent has about facing life as an adult. Usually, it is the parents – on behalf of the adolescent, the front line of society – who bear the brunt of the growing pains of their adolescent offspring.

· · · · · · · · · ·

If you have never been hated by your child,
you have never been a parent.

Bette Davis

· · · · · · · · · ·

Just as the call of adulthood presents challenges to young people, the manifestations of adolescence in children call for an adjustment by parents. In simplified terms, the child needs to mature and the parents need to relinquish sovereignty and, often, to look honestly at their own marital relationship. This last point may be surprising, but much adolescent misbehaviour can be traced to a lack of authentic love between the father and mother. In both cases growth is called for, and both need to learn to look toward their own tasks, to honour the other's process, and to stop pointing the finger in the belief that the other is the cause of all the family's misery. For many, especially if the household has not been functioning in a healthy manner previously, this period can be full of anger and resentment. Resolution, introspection, and communication are called for, but egos – bent on winning, or insisting they are right – get in the way.

The courtship period

Another ingredient adding confusion to the mix is that the period of adolescence usually corresponds with the time of searching for a partner. Sometimes, getting into a relationship is a way by which the adolescent seeks escape from the tensions and confusion he or she feels at home. This becomes, in almost all cases, a way of jumping out of the frying pan into the fire. The adolescent should recognize the danger of doing this, and the parents should be awake to the reality that if home is full of stress and pain, falling into premature intimate relationships is just one of the many destructive forms of escape their child is likely to seek out.

The troubles which many adolescents and their parents experience are signs of unfinished business: unresolved issues and hurts, resentment over past mistakes and injustices, immaturity (not always on the part of the adolescent), too much interference, too much distance and a plethora of other possibilities. These issues often come to a head when the young person starts looking towards marriage. One issue, which may arise now for the first time, is the tendency for many parents to feel that almost no one is good enough for their child. They have given their all for that child and, even though there may have been struggles over childrearing, one or both of them may be unable to see their child in an unbiased way, or to see their child's partner in anything other than a negative light.

Non-interference

Given the above backdrop, one boundary clarification pertaining to courtship which can be helpful to all parties at this point is given in the Bahá'í teachings. It is **not** the role of the parents to choose for their child whom he or she should marry. The time when parents selected partners for their children has, according to the Bahá'í writings, clearly come to an end and this is something for all parents who embrace the requirements of this new age to come to terms with. Yes, it opens the door to the possibility that the young person may make reckless decisions when seeking out a marriage partner, but as we have seen, making choices is one of the unique and crucial aspects of being human. Interestingly, according to Harville Hendrix, opening the door of free choice for courting young people makes it more likely that they will find a partner who will challenge them psychologically and emotionally in ways that give them the opportunity to awaken to their shadow self and heal wounds from their upbringing. This **is** a huge added challenge to the institution of marriage, but one that Hendrix maintains we should welcome. In the Bahá'í view, once the choice has been made parents do have a crucial role to play which can help preclude serious mistakes from being made, and this will be covered below.

If the relationship between the young person and the parents has been healthy, and the relationship between the parents is also good, and if the child has been raised with spiritual principles, then these kinds of issues will have been discussed and cleared up; usually, even if new ones arise, they are able to deal with them and resolve them. Unfortunately, these conditions seem to be the exception rather than the rule, leaving distance and misunderstandings between parents and their children at a time when if marriage is being contemplated, support, understanding, wisdom and clarity are most needed. This is because all parties will inevitably be going through a significant transition. Boundaries and alliances will be shifting, and if there is lack of unity the already challenging prospects of marriage may become mired in crossgenerational problems as well.

The role of parents before the wedding

As implied by the discussion above, parents have to be ready to shift gears when their children reach puberty. They need to learn about the physiological effects of puberty in order to understand some of the vagaries of their adolescent's behaviour. They need also to give space for their children to grow into adulthood. This doesn't mean hands off. Young people need their parents as much as ever, but usually in a somewhat transformed way. Often, especially in Western countries, there is a tendency for parents to be too hands off with respect to their adolescent children, leaving them to their own and society's devices. But parents at this stage do often need to let go of minor issues, so as to have credibility in addressing the larger issues. Too much involvement, without recognizing the need for young people to make their own choices and learn from their mistakes, can be anathema. If a young person has been brought up with a spiritual orientation and within a religious community, then at the stage of adolescence these can continue to be a source of guidance when he or she is perhaps less inclined to look towards parents for counsel.

Parents also need to recognize that extreme behaviour in their adolescent child is often a way of bringing attention to what is not working within the home, and this often means the marital relationship. If this message can be heeded and acted upon, the parents do far more for their adolescent than any other manifestation of 'concern'. Looking towards the crucial role of their own relationship and at their own character, and freeing themselves of their preconceived image of what their child should be, does a lot to allow the adolescent to grow into maturity without the stereotypical 'I'll show you' attitude.

Then there is the moment a young person first presents his or her intention or desire to get married. This is a highly charged moment whose gravity is usually felt by all parties. Parents want their children to have a good marriage, to make a wise choice; and children want their parents to accept the one they love so much. Hopefully the parents will already have been well informed about their potential son- or daughter-in-law, and their child will have had many discussions with them about their potential future spouse. It is generally helpful for the young couple to keep their parents abreast with developments in their relationship, letting them in on the process at an early stage and introducing them before getting too involved. If the parents are given time together with their potential son- or daughter-in-law, all parties will have a chance to get to know one another. With this backdrop, everyone concerned will be more ready to step into this new stage with understanding and unity.

The need for unity

Sometimes parents really do not like the choice of partner their child has made and fear for their child's and their potential grandchildren's future. In Western societies, parents generally think that they should just swallow the concerns they have, bite the bullet and do the best they can to live with their child's choice. Unfortunately, these kinds of misgivings have ways of cropping up in the form of interference or unconscious opposition after the couple has married. Sometimes, too, the choice **is** a bad one or their child may not be ready to marry, and the parents can see this with more clarity than the young couple. What should the parents do?

Consent of the parents

• • • • • • • • • •

*This great law He has laid down to strengthen
the social fabric,
to knit closer the ties of the home,
to place a certain gratitude and respect in the hearts
of the children
for those who have given them life
and sent their souls out on the eternal journey towards
their Creator.*

Shoghi Effendi

• • • • • • • • • •

There is a law in the Bahá'í Faith that the parents of a couple who wish to get married need to give their consent to the marriage before the wedding can take place. As stated above, parents have no right to interfere with the choice of partner their children make, but once made, their consent is essential. Consent is required from all living natural parents in every case where either party to the proposed marriage is a Bahá'í. There are, of course, hugely important demands embedded within this law. The parents need to familiarize themselves with the character of their child's desired partner and examine their situation without prejudice, sensitive to the huge disappointment to both if consent is withheld or postponed. The young couple needs to be prepared to defer to what may be their parents' last remnant of sovereignty in relation to them. These demands can be painful, but the pain is minimal compared to the pain and wounds engendered by a failed marriage. Beyond this, the process everyone needs to go through because of this call for parental consent can be healing in itself. Much unfinished business which might otherwise have been neglected can, if all parties play their part maturely, establish a much firmer base for future success in marriage and extended family relationships.

Before marriage, the most important human bonds we have are those between us and our parents. After marriage the most significant tie is that between us and our spouse. This conscious and formal giving of parental consent in this profound passage is like the passing of a baton; a clear signal that this dramatic shift is supported by all significant players.

· · · · · · · · · ·

I should have known something was wrong with my first wife,
when I brought her home to meet my parents –
they approved of her, y'know –my dog died,
that's what happened.

Woody Allen

· · · · · · · · · ·

For parents whose children are not Bahá'ís, the role is not so clear. This Bahá'í law requiring consent encourages greater consciousness and maturity with respect to family ties and thoughts about marriage. Bahá'í children are aware of this law from the beginning and are more likely to pay attention to involving their parents at earlier stages of courtship and to keeping their relationship with their parents open, respectful, and loving. These are qualities that are often missing in modern societies – and when they are missing this does not auger well for a future family life. Wise parents are going to be mindful of the seriousness of preparing their children for marriage and discussing all the important issues with them as they are growing.

The parents' perspective

In many ways, parents relive their own lives through their children. Watching their children grow, they remember their own development as children, but now through the conscious eyes of adults. There are, of course, myriad unconscious patterns being played out in this process. Consciousness is relative and is something that tends to grow generation after generation. When young people marry and have children, they begin yet another cycle of added consciousness. But for the parents, a circle is being closed. Their child has gone through the stages of babyhood, childhood, and adolescence, and is now embarking on the adult journey of getting married and having children of his or her own.

· · · · · · · · · ·

When I was a boy of 14, my father was so ignorant
I could hardly stand to have the old man around.
But when I got to be 21,
I was astonished at how much the old man had learned in
seven years.

Mark Twain

· · · · · · · · · ·

There is a tendency for adolescents to view their upbringing and their parents critically. Once married, the parents can sit back a bit and observe their own children struggling with many of the same kinds of challenges they themselves have had. Hopefully, the newer generation will have more consciousness and fewer imperfections, but the world will also have changed, creating greater complexities and new challenges. The parent's task is not over, but the largest part of the chore as parents has been completed and a new stage now begins for them.

*** *** ***

But now, before we move into the final stages of the single person's quest to find a partner, as well as the transition into the state of marriage, some steps need to be retraced. I want to pick up some threads from Chapter 1 and go deeper into the question of self-knowledge. Bringing to completion some of the concepts introduced there will better lead into looking at the final steps to marriage.

13

Towards Completion

In the opening chapter we looked at the various aspects of what it means to be a human being. Now I want to pick up on some of these facets of human uniqueness, see how they relate to each other, and go psychologically deeper into an understanding of who we are and what motivates us to marry. We are at the threshold of having come full circle, and this necessitates a deeper, more comprehensive, view of who we are and what we are about.

We saw in our opening chapter that we are, in essence, a soul with a spiritual quest. We come into this world with an exalted but undiscovered purpose. We are increasingly able to look back upon the development of the universe and see that until humans came into being there was no aspect of this creative process which could look back upon itself or upon the process. With the human creature, consciousness of self and the ability to explore our origins was born. In the Bahá'í writings we are told that the universe is not complete without the human. Yet, having come into the world with its material demands and, having developed an ego as a necessary vehicle for coming into self-awareness, we are stymied.

Problems of the ego

Our ego seems to have an insatiable appetite and desire for the things of this world. At the same time, human socialization eventuates in the development of a shadow self. The ego presents itself to the world with a face which is incomplete and replete with buried, unconscious elements which seem to impede higher development. If it is honest with itself, our ego will recognize that it is transcended and, without finding its higher purpose, is in a state of acute existential anxiety. When our ego recognizes its situation in all honesty – a recognition which may always be there but buried in our unconscious – it becomes a conscious seeker for its higher purpose. In other words, recognition of its soul's needs kicks in.

Although human intention or will represents a crowning achievement in evolution, it is, in and of itself, comparatively weak when it comes to instituting its own development. The finite mind cannot comprehend the Infinite. When it seeks to overcome its ego desires, it falls into traps and tends to go in circles. 'Abdu'l-Bahá explains this conundrum of our egos in this way:

> Just as the earth attracts everything to the centre of gravity, and every object thrown into space will come down, so also material ideas and worldly thoughts attract man to the centre of self. Anger, passion, ignorance, prejudice, greed, envy, covetousness, jealousy and suspicion prevent man from ascending to the realms of holiness, imprisoning him in the claws of self and the cage of egotism. The physical man, unassisted by the divine power, trying to escape from one of these invisible enemies, will unconsciously fall into the hands of another. No sooner does he attempt to soar upward than the density of the love of self, like the power of gravity, draws him to the centre of the earth.

The Source

This is where the soul, seeking its own development, cannot side-step the religious question. The highest intention of the ego is, ironically, to recognize its Creative Source and submit to its will. This enables our souls to tap into a source of power which transcends the limits and drawbacks of our human inheritance. Here, the purely human capacity of intention, already the highest outcome of evolution, interfaces with the Creative Force which originated it, lending a whole new and massive impetus to its development. This interface takes place through the agency of what the Bahá'í writings refer to as the Manifestation of God. These are those paradigmatic figures already referred to, who have founded the worlds' great religions.

Let me draw an analogy. A plant always grows first under the ground. Eventually the seed, which has first germinated in the soil, shoots up and finds the light of day for the first time. But finding enough light can be a problem for the budding plant. If it is too much in the shade, if it is blocked by other plants or objects and never actually gets exposed to the sun, it may become stunted or even wither and die. If, however, in its struggle, it finally comes into contact with the light of the sun, the energy from the sun will stimulate its growth as never before, enabling the plant to become full and strong. Analogously, the plant's shooting up from underneath the soil can represent the emergence of self, our ability to choose for ourselves what we will now do. But if the plant does not find the light of the sun, its efforts to grow will eventually dissipate – this representing the efforts of our egos. If the plant, however, finds the light of the sun – which is actually its creative source and represents in this analogy, **our** Creative Source – the connection of the plant to the sunlight will serve to draw the plant up, filling out its development as would otherwise be impossible. The plant, 'finding' the sun is like our soul finding its Creator. It is analogous to the emergence of the faithful self or believer whose existence and life, according to Bahá'u'lláh, 'are to be regarded as the originating purpose of all creation'.

Primal concerns and marriage

Discovering our Creative Source is not, however, the end of our journey. Rather, it is the conscious beginning of our spiritual path.

Our primal beginnings, even from a scientific point of view, are one. Everything in the universe is a revealed portion of the universe's primal oneness. It is the task of humans to realize oneness, to achieve unity, which is a reflection of this primal oneness. Thus, the programme of the great paradigmatic figures has always been to help bring us into relationship with each other in ever-widening circles and with ever-increasing degrees of consciousness. In these times, it is the crying need of humanity to find unity on a global scale. This path has guideposts which are provided by these same Manifestations – and this brings us back to the question of marriage. If we are to be in harmony with humanity in all its diversity, we need to start by developing a profoundly deep and abiding relationship with one different other. This is the essence of marriage – it becomes the training ground for our relationship with ever-wider circles of different others. While marriage is a relationship with only one other, it makes up in depth what it lacks in number. We need to learn the difficult lessons which the intimate bonds of marriage present us with and this will help us in all our other human relationships.

The human journey

In order to reach some understanding of the nature of the difficult lessons in marriage and how best to prepare ourselves for them, we need to go a bit deeper into our own individual development and psychological backgrounds. Each human being begins its journey as a 'sorry germ' (Qur'án), or single fertilized cell which divides, multiplies, and diversifies, reflecting in its various stages of development much of the biological evolution on this planet. In fact, much like the universe itself, we start as a single unified point with untold potential folded up within us. Through our life in our mother's womb we lived in a protected, warm, aquatic environment. Completely taken care of, we floated blissfully through momentous stages of growth which mirrored billions of years of development on this planet. A revolution occurred when we passed on our birthday from the world of the matrix into the wide, air-filled variable climate of the world outside the womb.

· · · · · · · · · ·

I was caesarean born. You can't really tell, although whenever
I leave a house,
I go out through the window.

Steven Wright

· · · · · · · · · ·

Though the conditions of our environment had changed dramatically, the fact of our being cared for and nurtured did not, at least not right away. Perhaps all that really changed in this respect was that we had to cry out from time to time (or perhaps often) to make our needs known. This little creature, while in the womb and for months after our birthday, was not yet a self-aware human. We did not distinguish ourselves from our environment. We just 'were'. While in the womb, our experience was that of oneness. Once we were born we gradually came to be aware of an 'out there' but it was an 'out there' that took care of all we required. Whatever it was that was out there answered our cries for attention, at least initially, and usually even anticipated our needs. Insofar as there was a world outside of us, we experienced ourselves as its Regent, as a little king or queen in complete control.

· · · · · · · · · ·

A perfect example of minority rule is a baby in the house.

Anonymous

· · · · · · · · · ·

Dethronement

In time, a massive shift in our awareness occurred which, though we do not recall it, continues to have a momentous impact on our experience of the world. As we continued to develop as an infant, to develop co-ordination, to become mobile, to begin to speak, our caregivers started to expect us to do some things on our own. However gently or gradually this was done, there came a time when we – small monarch that we were – took this as a slap in the face, a supreme insult. In fact, we came to recognize that those others who had been anticipating most of our wishes and who hurried to respond to our every cry actually had a will of their own which was independent of our own wishes. More and more it became clear that they intended to impose **their** will on **us**. Not only had we, the monarch, become subordinate: as we woke up to our true situation we came to realize we were **absolutely** dependent. It became clearer and clearer that those beings who still spent much of their time looking after our needs could, in fact, choose **not** to look after us – and this was a powerfully frightening realization. From that moment, the now much more aware little creature that we were started to check and test its caregivers to see if they were really serious about their job.

. . . .

We spend the first twelve months of our children's lives
teaching them to walk and talk
and the next twelve years telling them to sit down
and shut up.

Phyllis Diller

. . . .

I refer to this significant development as the 'dethronement'. The nascent creature that we were has moved from its blissful state of being and feeling at one – a description which sounds much like what Buddhists refer to as Enlightenment or Nirvana – to the painful, even dreadful, awareness of otherness. Ironically, this supremely trying lesson is actually necessary in order for us to develop a sense of self. For our caregivers, however, apart from noticing the development of a definite negative attitude in their young one, most of the significance of what occurred has probably been lost on them. Our parents or other caregivers have, after all, seen us all along as a distinct being who needs their attention but will grow up gradually to be responsible for itself, once we have learned the various skills of being human.

• • • • • • • • • •

Go directly – see what she's doing,
and tell her she mustn't.

Anonymous

• • • • • • • • • •

Since these are largely pre-verbal developments that take place when our conscious awareness is still nascent, these experiences – both of the primal oneness and the dethronement – do not become part of our conscious memory. Although we have all been through this, none of us recall it. Still, the feelings and associations remain deeply etched in our 'old brain', that part of our brain which apparently does not have much to do with our ability for abstract thinking but 'contains' and records significant experiences in 'feeling' form. In our later life, more conscious experiences – our feelings of connectedness or closeness to others – will to some degree echo the experience of primal oneness; conversely, feelings of insecurity, of vulnerability and strangeness, will tend to evoke the terrible feelings associated with our dethronement and the fear of death.

This painful 'adjustment' to the human world has happened to all of us, no matter how good our caregivers were. In cases where caregivers were less than very good, all kinds of other issues and anxieties were born in this period, issues involving trust and separation anxieties, for example. And we all deal with these issues – or, rather mask them – in our own unique ways. This all becomes part of the largely unconscious baggage that we will carry into our marriages as adults, where we will have the painful opportunities of dealing with them more consciously (although our tendency will be to remain unconscious).

Recapitulation

Now we can begin to see how our unconscious mechanisms relate to both the development of our soul and to our marriage. Our nascent experience of primal oneness is analogous to the primal 'seed' of the universe, also to the Garden of Eden described in Genesis. Our birth is akin to the 'Big Bang' that propelled the universe on its course, eventuating in human consciousness which has the potential to reflect this whole development and to create and experience unity through our connectedness. Our dethronement, in relation to the story of Adam and Eve is, of course, analogous to their expulsion from the Garden of Eden for having eaten from the Tree of Knowledge. This 'event' set humans on the path whereon we are required to seek out our Creator consciously, and learn to relate to each other in all our diversity and to develop bonds of unity.

Thus, our soul – our essence - is on a journey. In this world it needs to be in close association with an ego capable of making choices. The development of this ego, as we have seen, comes about through the process of socialization which, as a by-product, leaves us with plenty of unconscious baggage. Also, our egos are not complete. As social creatures we seek out relationships with others and this serves our development. The more we associate with others the more we fill out as individuals. Our potential is called into being through contact with people different from ourselves and we crave this filling out. However, the closer we get to others, the more likely we are to call our unconscious issues to the surface. When we get **very** close to another, so close that our ego barriers break down, we experience intense feelings of love. This is romance, which we have discussed in the chapter on falling in love. The ecstasy we feel when in love is thus a reflection of our prenatal experience of primal oneness.

· · · · · · · · · ·

When I grow up, I want to be a little boy.

Joseph Heller

· · · · · · · · · ·

However, following on the heels of this, when we come down to earth and see that the human we are in love with has all kinds of unconscious baggage which presents itself to us in the most maddening of ways, we again fall from this feeling of grace, make our exit from the garden of delights, and start to evoke the deep feelings associated with our early dethronement. These are the worlds we enter when we choose to marry.

Psychologically, this presents a supreme challenge. But these challenges serve the growth of our soul, especially if we are ready to see them as doing that. In marriage, our issues and those of our spouse are most effectively brought to the surface, allowing them to be dealt with and profound growth to occur. How this is done is beyond the scope of this book but if, in full consciousness, we are aware that this is what an authentic marital relationship entails and we are open to and welcoming of this opportunity, we are in the best position to reap the most gains. In fact, the marital relationship – because it so deep, because it is meant to endure, and because there is no healthy escape from it – serves our growth to such a degree that it is almost irreplaceable. People who choose not to marry must seek out a path that challenges them spiritually in order to try to make up for what they are missing in not getting married.

As we are social creatures, we can see that as single human beings we are not complete. The whole world with all its diverse peoples has in this age become our crucible. The individual soul ever seeks relationship; its path to completion involves all, for our source is one and we are all connected. The most basic coming together is the marital union. Our feeling of not being complete is more conscious when we lack a partner and that, in my opinion, is why marriage – although outwardly a social and material arrangement – is an eternal teaching, present in all the religions of the past and which, according to 'Abdu'l-Bahá, will continue to be promulgated in future dispensations. This is also why the demands on marriage are much greater in this present age, for it must now enshrine the principles of equality, the elimination of prejudice, the individual's responsibility to seek out truth for his or her own self and the shouldering of co-responsibility for the development of the institutions for a new age.

We can now see how it is that when we are about to embark on the journey of marriage we are taking a most momentous step. This is why we need to develop more consciousness in the process of knowing ourselves and finding a partner. This is why we need to take care about how we spend time with people. This is why we need to control our primitive impulses. With this background, I want to take us into the final chapter, which is getting engaged and getting married.

14

Taking the Step

· · · · · · · · · ·

Thou art even as a finely tempered sword
concealed in the darkness of its sheath
and its value hidden from the artificer's knowledge.
Wherefore come forth from the sheath of self and desire
that thy worth may be made resplendent
and manifest unto all the world.

Bahá'u'lláh

· · · · · · · · · ·

Have we covered everything we need to know in order to prepare ourselves for marriage? I very much doubt it. We are complex creatures and, as I have pointed out, our societies are in a transitional phase. We have not yet found a paradigm for a healthy new world order, so the complexities are multiplied. But we are called to develop as much consciousness and maturity as we reasonably can – we cannot wait for perfection. In fact, most of the perfecting will necessarily come after the wedding. Most of our self-knowledge will also come after marriage. Ultimately, we need to be courageous and decisive. In this concluding chapter, we will look at engagement, the wedding, the honeymoon, and briefly forward into the first steps of transition into the state of being married. But let me first offer two possible models of courtship which could replace the present, largely faulty, one. I put these forward tentatively, merely as possibilities. They are largely idealized but offer a view of where we might be heading socially when we have a more conscious orientation.

· · · · · · · · · ·

If you want to find out some things about yourself –
and in vivid detail, too –
just try calling your wife fat.

P. J. O'Rourke

· · · · · · · · · ·

Model 1: Waiting until you are really ready

Ideally, from the earliest years of our development our parents are helping to prepare us for marriage. They do this by providing a loving and spiritual atmosphere to home life, encouraging the development of virtues and a love for our Creator, being just and loving parents, keeping lines of communication open and solving problems of family life together. As we get older, our parents ideally talk to us about sexuality and relationships, giving wise guidance, helping us to under-stand the connection between our present attitudes and actions and our future life as married adults. Beginning from our earliest aware-ness that we are responsible for our own spiritual development, we look toward developing and readying ourselves for marriage. We do not put off the needed steps toward preparing ourselves for marriage, because these developments take time.

We do not get married until we feel a solid and confident sense of self and knowledge of our purpose in life. And there are goals towards which we can strive, all of which serve to help ready us for marriage. These include getting further education, developing employment skills, honing artistic talents and athletic abilities, and finding ways to serve humanity which will lead us to experience the diversity and oneness of the human race and the need for equality and justice in the world. All this can be done without getting involved in intimate relationships, yet will move us towards the maturity and vision we will need as a marriage partner. In fact, falling in love can distract us from many of these important tasks and thus serve to inhibit our development, lengthening the time we need to properly prepare ourselves or, even more seriously, trapping us into a relationship which we don't want to leave but do not have the maturity to handle.

In this model, we proceed with our lives in a conscious, mature way, preparing ourselves for our adult life, befriending others, spending time in groups with our peers, conversing with members of the opposite sex, getting to know the differences between men and women, learning to see beyond the masks which people present, but not getting intimately involved until we feel ready to make serious moves toward marriage. If we take this path, we need to discipline our minds not to get distracted by constantly contemplating relationships and fantasizing involvements. This of course, can be hard to do, especially if most in our circle of friends are all involved in close, perhaps sexual, relationships. It can help to find a circle of friends who at least respect your values and choices, more helpful if you have friends who share your values.

Limiting time spent with the opposite sex to group events and encounters helps to lighten the pressure for intimate involvement. Still, taking this path requires clarity and the ability to articulate your approach to others, especially to those members of the opposite sex who want to get more involved with you. Taking this path, however, should not be seen as an ascetic, monk-like existence. It is important and helpful to be around others, to have kind and affectionate relationships with your own family, and also amongst your friends. Being involved in various disciplines and studies helps keep you on your path but you should not neglect the people element in your life either.

In this model, when you do feel it is time to seek out a marriage it is not necessary to contemplate a long courtship, because you have already developed the maturity and vision. All the steps described in this book can be covered adequately in a period of months rather than years. This model is very different from the dating and relationship scene currently found in the Western world, so your family and friends may find it very strange, even reckless, for you to consider marrying someone you have only been close to for a few months.

Model 2: The long courtship

Neil Clark Warren, a Christian psychologist referred to earlier, believes that longer courtships are the best approach to successful marriages. He cites statistics showing that the longer you hold off marrying, the more likely you will be successful in marriage. Being Christian, he believes that having sex before marriage is not right, but he does not go into much discussion about it. This lack of discussion is a bit troublesome, because having a long courtship (and he is talking about years) begs the question about the difficulty in holding off sexual involvement.

Spending a long time together with one person, dating that person, getting to know that person, spending time together sharing thoughts and dreams – falling in love becomes all but inevitable. And when we are in love with a person with whom we spend a lot of time, strong sexual attraction also becomes inevitable. The presence of sexual attraction does **not** mean that a couple have to become sexually involved, but if they permit themselves to be physically close to each other, and show physical affection through hugging, kissing and making out, then some degree of sexual involvement is already taking place, even if the couple restrain themselves from having intercourse. Furthermore, the temptation to go further, once the ball is rolling, becomes harder and harder to resist. Wisdom is needed here, and the usual manner of young lovers expressing their love through physical affection is not recommended.

If, for whatever reason, you do not feel ready to marry but you want to be involved in a close relationship with someone and draw it out until you feel you are ready for marriage, then the way to do this is to agree with one another to consciously avoid physical forms of showing affection. This, like Model 1, may be hard for other people to understand, so you both will need to be clear about why you are doing this and able to explain it to others. In some cultural environments – usually religious environments – this may not be necessary, but in most Western social circles the standards of courtship are very different from this.

Support from extended family

When maturity is not the central issue, but practical and financial concerns seem to prevent a couple from marrying, one option is to seek support from parents. For example, if both of you are still studying and are unable to support yourselves, but you otherwise feel ready to marry, parents may be included in the picture and decide that they will support your getting married and provide funds until you can get on your own feet financially. This kind of arrangement can work, but it takes maturity and detachment for all parties. Often with money goes the implication of power; parents may feel that because they are footing the bill they should have say in other matters. These boundary issues need to be clarified from the start. It also goes without saying that this kind of relationship should not be extended any longer than necessary; that the young couple should be as responsible as possible financially and become independent as soon as they can.

Proposal

. . . .

I'm going crazy.
Want to come along?

Anonymous

. . . .

Once you have found someone whose character you have become well acquainted with, whom you can have intimate dialogue with, who is attractive to you, who meets the most essential criteria of what you want in a mate, with whom you feel capable of building a life and family, and – beyond this – the parents are all pleased, then it is time to get married. The climactic point of the courting process, as traditionally seen in the movies, is the marriage proposal. It may not always be like it is in the movies, and it need not be. It may be more of a mutual agreement than an actual proposal. Whatever form it takes, once the decision to marry has been made by a couple, the manner of their relationship will become transformed.

Engagement

The engagement period has often come to be long and drawn out. This is not needed if the couple is really ready when they decide to marry and, if they have decided to marry, they should be ready! However, although it need not be long, the engagement period is likely to intensify feelings, and some of the many elements that make up married life will start to appear. Family members will be involved because wedding plans need to be made. Plans about where to live, finances, finishing studies, leaving or finding jobs, and so on, come to the fore and need to be dealt with.

During the engagement, the gravity of marriage starts to take hold, and feelings of love come to be expressed more openly. The couple is coming to terms with each other in a more serious way and, at the same time, each one is coming to terms with marriage in a more serious way. Plans for the wedding and differences over what each one wants for the wedding often bring many challenges into focus. This can be a period of extremes, sometimes confusing, where the ball seems to be moving unavoidably on while doubts may start to surface.

While this setting of the stage for marriage is much like marriage in many respects, one thing needs to be pointed out:

• • • • • • • • • •

My fiancé and I are having a little disagreement.
What I want is a big church wedding
with bridesmaids and flowers and a no-expense-spared
reception;
and what he wants is to break off our engagement.

Sally Poplin

• • • • • • • • • •

engagement is **not** marriage. During this time, essential issues may surface which have not been anticipated and these **may** call into question the wisdom of the marriage. These issues must be confronted and dealt with as openly as possible. Usually the tendency to get 'cold feet' after an engagement is a sign of our tendency to escape (see Chapter 5). In rare cases, serious factors that have been suppressed come to the surface. This may be a difficult time to think about changing one's mind, because of all the expectations that surround the announcement of marriage plans, but the couple will especially need to express themselves openly and listen empathetically to each other. Although painful and complicated, it is much better to call off a wedding than to get a divorce. But because the unconscious urge to escape can be profound, if a couple are already engaged to be married I would advise enlisting the help of a therapist to explore these issues before calling all plans off.

The wedding

Marriage is both a tradition and something new. It has been around for a long time and every culture has developed traditions around the marriage ceremony. On the other hand, the world has become quite a different place in recent times and no single tradition embraces all the changes. Couples marry across cultures, traditions, religions, and ethnicity, and new ways of doing almost everything have emerged. The contemporary wedding ceremony should be seen as a kind of bridge between the bride and the groom, their respective families, their traditions, and the spirit of the time.

There has become a trend for many couples to design their ceremony according to their own tastes and to exclude their parents from the process. Of course, a couple are going to want a ceremony which represents what they believe about marriage, but that does not mean parents need to be excluded. When differences of religion or culture are present within or between families, much can be done to include different elements to make everyone feel good about taking part. In fact, if the couple takes on the whole responsibility for organizing everything the pressure can be intense, and the honeymoon will feel more like a period of recovery than the beginning of a new life. In most traditions, the families of the couple getting married have a role and most parents like to feel this kind of responsibility.

Much can be said about weddings. There are a huge variety of possibilities. Some are lavish and extremely expensive; some are as simple as can be. I personally favour simplicity, but there is a place for (almost) everything. Some families and some traditions expect to have a lavish wedding and in some cases this is appropriate. Sometimes however, high-priced affairs are organized against all practical reasoning, pushing families into debt or using resources that could have been better used in getting the young couple started. I will not go into this issue in any depth because, really, it is a matter for the couple and their families to decide. All parties should be prepared to make compromises, though, because of the wide variety and mixture of approaches in our pluralistic reality.

The newly weds

Since the approach taken to courtship in this book is far from the norm these days, at least a few things need to be said about the beginning period of marriage for a couple who have approached courtship more or less as recommended. Compared to most contemporary couples, the newly weds who have approached courtship with a spiritual mindset can be contrasted in a few significant ways. They know each other deeply in terms of character, but in terms of living habits and other day-to-day considerations there may be quite a few surprises. Furthermore, they should have developed a deep capacity for verbal intimacy but in terms of sexual intimacy they are inexperienced, at least with each other.

Becoming accustomed

· · · · · · · · · ·

It's just like magic. When you live by yourself, all by yourself, all your annoying habits are gone!

Merrill Markoe

· · · · · · · · · ·

Almost everyone has a way of being with others which contrasts with how they are at home. We are not used to having our home living habits scrutinized. Our family of origin may have had things to say about our personal idiosyncrasies, but by and large they have either become accustomed to them or they share them! But our new bride or groom may be quite as surprised at our behaviour around the house as we are at his or hers. It takes time to become accustomed to these kinds of differences, especially if we haven't had much experience sharing living quarters with other people in the past. You will develop home routines and habits as a couple, but this takes time. The lesson here is to take that time. If there are behaviours which you find unacceptable you can speak up, but don't make it a 'Change or I'm going home to mother' issue.

· · · · · · · · · ·

Bad quarrels come when two people are wrong.
Worse quarrels come when two people are right.

Betty Smith

· · · · · · · · · ·

If neither one of you has had sexual experience, first of all, be glad. Innocence is the best starting point. In Canada, one study found that most people – even liberally minded people – actually prefer the idea of having a partner without sexual experience to one with lots of experience. Review the chapters on sex and love if you find this puzzling.

One of the benefits of the sexual revolution that we can all share is that we have no reason to feel that sex is bad or wrong in itself – at least not for a married couple. One negative side-effect of the sexual revolution for chaste newly-weds is the way sex is portrayed in movies and other media. These images give a distorted view of love-making and it would be of great benefit if you could throw out any such images you may have picked up from these sources. Let yourselves enjoy the spirit of discovery and take your time! You have a lifetime to get to know each other sexually. Don't worry about performance. Being chaste brings with it a certain amount of shyness about sex which is natural. This is one aspect of sexual encounter which can be beautiful but is rarely portrayed in movies. In the God-given context of marriage you can feel good about sexual exploration and can gradually let go of being coy.

· · · · · · · · · ·

Why do women fake orgasms?
Because men fake foreplay.

Anonymous

· · · · · · · · · ·

Marriage takes more adjustment than most people are aware of, and it is partly because of this that the early years are usually the most difficult. The kinds of difficulties you may encounter, and their solutions, are far beyond the scope of this book, but it helps to know that struggles are almost inevitable. Be prepared for challenges and be open to getting help if things seem to be falling apart.

The path of marriage

· · · · · · · · · ·

If it weren't for marriage,
men and women would have to fight with total strangers.

Anonymous

· · · · · · · · · ·

We enter marriage as two individuals with distinct backgrounds, tastes, habits, beliefs, hang-ups, dreams, and capacities. But we are not complete. Hopefully, there is much that we share in common that will help bind us together. And there are likely to be significant differences which will challenge this bond, but from which we can learn some of life's most significant lessons.

In marriage, we move from the theoretical and ideal to the concrete and real. We live life together. Often one wants more closeness while the other wants more time alone. These kinds of basic differences will bring up issues that have to do with our upbringing and childhood experiences, and such encounters can be surprising and hurtful. Those that have an unconscious basis will be the most difficult to come to terms with but this is what, psychologically speaking, marriage is all about. If we can face these issues and learn from them, we move towards wholeness and authentic liberation. This is not a freedom from the other, but the liberation that comes with unity.

· · · · · · · · · ·

Basically my wife was immature.
I'd be at home in the bath and she'd come in
and sink my boats.

Woody Allen

· · · · · · · · · ·

The realm of the spirit

Much of this book has been premised on the fact that we are essentially spiritual beings. God has given us a limited span to live on this earth, and as we live out these years we go through various phases in our life. The period when we are searching for a mate is one of these; being married and having children is another. At all stages of our life, we are engaged and involved with other human beings, but our marriage partner is the most special. Searching for that partner is probably the most exciting quest. But in both the searching and the finding we must always remember that the most encompassing and significant relationship of all is the one we have with our Creator.

But God wants us to marry. He wants us to love one another, and the marital bond is the prototype of our love for others. Marriage is thus a spiritual institution with a spiritual purpose. The main purpose of marriage is to have children; not just any children, but children who recognize God. Beyond that, another purpose is for the husband and wife to 'ever improve the spiritual life of each other'. Marriage is for the creation of spiritually cognizant children and a spiritually developed mother and father. These are the essentials.

All of this has a practical bearing and takes place in the concrete day-to-day settings of our life. But when we recognize these spiritual needs, we begin to fathom the spiritual significance of finding a marriage partner. The path to finding a partner is thus primarily a spiritual path. This means keeping spiritual principle before us at all times. Insofar as we can do this, we will be confirmed, even if it seems like we are not making headway. Insofar as we let our own desires and attractions take precedence, we are going backwards, even if it seems like we are having fun and success.

Because of its spiritual nature, we are bound to be spiritually tested on the path of finding a mate. Perhaps the quintessential test – one that will be put before us in various guises – is the test of 'Whom are we attracted to more, a potential partner with whom we may carry out our spiritual purpose, or God, the Master of the Universe, who created us and established our purpose?' This is sometimes a test of will, a test of discernment, a test of consciousness, a test of steadfastness, a test of authenticity, a test of vigilance, a test of humility, a test of faithfulness, a test of courage, and the list goes on. We cannot know all of God's devices, but we know that nothing happens to us on His path that does not have meaning, and it is all for our perfecting. In this way, we can come full circle in everything we do, not the least of which is finding a partner.

• • • • • • • • • •

The more we search for ourselves, the less likely we are
to find ourselves,
and the more we search for God, and to serve our fellow-men,
the more profoundly will we become acquainted
with ourselves,
and the more inwardly assured.
This is one of the great spiritual laws of life.
Letter on behalf of Shoghi Effendi

• • • • • • • • • •

Once we have found a mate, the spiritual path continues in the practical setting of the home we make together. In a healthy marriage, the home becomes a place where we feel warmth, love, belonging, closeness, happiness, comfort, and joy. But these qualities of the home do not come automatically; rather, they usually take a lot of work. This is the kind of work which requires us to stretch ourselves and bring out of ourselves qualities which have always been there but needed to be jarred before we became aware of them. It is this jarring process which causes pain and often prompts us to want to lash out or escape. In order to build unity, we will need to recognize our own need for perfecting and to develop a different reflex to challenges to our ego. But this is not something to fear. Yes, we are here to develop our character and a healthy realistic outlook, and that is what this book has been all about. But the joy of marriage is truly worth all the preparation and pain that it may entail. And this joy is not only ours, but also our children's – and beyond them, all who enter our home and experience the environment created by a family founded on spiritual and physical unity.

· · · · · · · · · ·

My home is the home of peace.
My home is the home of joy and delight.
My home is the home of laughter and exaltation.
Whoever enters through the portals of this home,
must go out with gladsome heart.
This is the home of light;
whoever enters here must become illumined.

'Abdu'l-Bahá

· · · · · · · · · ·

Bibliography

'Abdu'l-Bahá. *Paris Talks: Addresses given by 'Abdu'l-Bahá in Paris 1911–1912*. London: Bahá'í Publishing Trust, 12th ed. 1995.

——. *The Promulgation of Universal Peace: Talks Delivered by 'Abdu'l-Bahá during His Visit to the United States and Canada in 1912*. Comp. Howard MacNutt. Wilmette, Ill.: Bahá'í Publishing Trust, 2nd ed. 1982.

——. *Selections from the Writings of 'Abdu'l-Bahá*. Comp. Research Department of The Universal House of Justice. Translated by a Committee at the Bahá'í World Centre and by Marzieh Gail. Haifa: Bahá'í World Centre, 1978.

——. *Some Answered Questions*. Collected and translated by Laura Clifford Barney. Wilmette, Ill.: Bahá'í Publishing Trust, 4th ed. 1981.

Angier, Natalie. *Woman: An Intimate Geography*. New York: Anchor Books, 2000.

Austen, Jane. *Pride and Prejudice* (1813). London: Penguin Classics, 1996.

Bahá'í Marriage and Family Life: Selections from the Writings of the Bahá'í Faith. National Spiritual Assembly of the Bahá'ís of Canada. Wilmette, Ill: Bahá'í Publishing Trust, 1983.

Bahá'í Readings: Selections from the Writings of The Báb, Bahá'u'lláh and 'Abdu'l-Bahá for Daily Meditation. National Spiritual Assembly of the Bahá'ís of Canada. Thornhill, Ontario: Bahá'í Canada, 2nd ed. 1985.

Bahá'u'lláh. *Gleanings from the Writings of Bahá'u'lláh.* Translated by Shoghi Effendi. Wilmette, Ill: Bahá'í Publishing Trust, 2nd ed. 1976.

—. *The Hidden Words.* Translated by Shoghi Effendi. Wilmette, Ill.: Bahá'í Publishing Trust, 1985.

—. *The Kitáb-i-Aqdas: The Most Holy Book.* Haifa: Bahá'í World Centre, 1992.

—. *Kitáb-i-Íqán: The Book of Certitude.* Translated by Shoghi Effendi. Wilmette, Ill.: Bahá'í Publishing Trust, 2nd ed. 1983.

—. *The Seven Valleys and the Four Valleys.* Translated by M. Gail and Ali-Kuli Khan. Wilmette, Ill.: Bahá'í Publishing Trust, 3rd ed. 1986.

—. *Tablets of Bahá'u'lláh Revealed after the Kitáb-i-Aqdas.* Comp. Research Department. Translated by Habib Taherzadeh et al. Wilmette, Ill: Bahá'í Publishing Trust, 2nd ed. 1978.

Balyuzi, H. M. *'Abdu'l-Bahá.* Oxford: George Ronald, 1971.

Becker, Ernest. *The Denial of Death.* New York: Macmillan, 1973.

Benson, A. C. *Escape and Other Essays* (1915). Reprinted by Kessinger Publishing Co., 2004.

Berger, Peter L. *The Social Construction of Reality: A Treatise in the Sociology of Knowledge.* Harmondsworth: Penguin Books, 1967.

Bibby, W. R., and Posterski, D. C. *The Emerging Generation.* Toronto: Irwin Publishing, 1985.

Bible, The New Oxford Annotated. Revised Standard Version. Oxford: Oxford University Press, 1977.

Blumenthal, Erik. *The Way to Inner Freedom.* Trans. Nancy Benvenga. Oxford: OneWorld, 1988.

Brandon, Nathaniel. *The Psychology of Romantic Love.* New York: Bantam, 1981.

Brooker, Catherine. *Balanced Living for Busy Bahá'ís.* Oxford: George Ronald, 2003.

Burns, David. *Feeling Good: The New Mood Therapy.* New York: Avon Books, 1992.

The Compilation of Compilations, Volumes I and II. Prepared by the Universal House of Justice 1963–1990. Maryborough, Victoria, Aus.: Bahá'í Publications Australia, 1991.

Conrad, Joseph. *Lord Jim* (1900).

Danesh, H. B. *Unity, the Creative Foundation of Peace.* Toronto: Fitzhenry-Whiteside, 1986.

Eliot, George. *Daniel Deronda* (1876).

Eliot, T. S. *The Complete Poems and Plays.* Orlando, Fl.: Harcourt, Brace and Co., 1980.

Erikson, Erik. *Childhood and Society.* New York: W. W. Norton and Co., 1950.

Ha elhagysz, veled mehetek? 1000 családias idézet. If you leave me, can I come too? Family quotes. Chosen, edited and translated by Gábor Salamon and Melinda Zalotaz. Budapest: Cartaphilus Kiadó, 2001.

Hendrix, Harville. *Getting the Love You Want: A Guide for Couples.* New York: Harper and Row, 1988.

—. *Keeping the Love You Find: A Personal Guide.* New York: Simon and Schuster, 1992.

Jaspers, Karl. *Way to Wisdom.* New Haven, Connecticut: Yale Univ. Press, 1954.

Johnson, Robert A. *We: Understanding the Psychology of Romantic Love.* New York: HarperCollins, 1983.

Laing, R. D. *The Politics of Experience.* Harmondsworth: Penguin, 1967.

Laszlo, Ervin. *Science and the Akashic Field: An Integral Theory of Everything.* Rochester, VT: Inner Traditions, 2004.

Lights of Guidance: A Bahá'í Reference File. Compiled by Helen Bassett Hornby. New Delhi: Bahá'í Publishing Trust, 1994.

May, Rollo. *Love and Will.* New York: Delta, 1969.

McLuhan, Marshall. *The Mechanical Bride* (1951). Reprinted Corte Madera, Calif: Gingko Press, 2001.

Michael, Robert T.; Gagnon, John H; Laumann, Edward O.; Kolata, Gina. *Sex in America: A Definitive Survey.* New York: Warner, 1995.

Napier, Augustus; Whitaker, Carl. *The Family Crucible: The Intense Experience of Family Therapy.* New York: HarperCollins, 1988.

Office for National Statistics, United Kingdom. *Social Trends 2006,* at www.statistics.gov.uk/social trends 36/.

Plato. *The Dialogues.* Apology. Trans. Benjamin Jowett.

Peck, M. Scott. *The Road Less Traveled: A New Psychology of Love, Traditional Values and Spiritual Growth.* New York: Simon and Schuster, 1978.

Qur'án. *The Meaning of the Glorious Qur'án.* Trans. M. M. Pickthall. Beirut: Dar Al-Kitab Allubnani, 1970.

Sahtouris, Elisabet. *Gaia: The Human Journey from Chaos to Cosmos.* New York: Simon and Schuster, 1989.

Shotter, John. 'The development of personal powers', in *The Integration of a Child into a Social World.* M.P.M.Richards (ed.). Cambridge: Cambridge University Press,1974.

Switzer, W. R. *Morality and Religious Contexts: A Study of the Attitudes of Catholic High School Students.* Unpublished Master's Thesis, University of Alberta, 1987.

Tolkien, J. R. R. *The Lord of the Rings.* London: George Allen and Unwin, 1955.

Warren, Neil Clark. *Finding the Love of Your Life.* Colorado: Focus on the Family, 1992.

Wollstonecraft, Mary. *A Vindication of the Rights of Women* (1797).

Vanier, Jean. *Becoming Human.* Toronto: House of Anansi, 1998.

References

NOTE FROM THE PUBLISHER: The Internet is both a blessing and a curse for authors and editors: a blessing in that it provides an almost inexhaustible source of quotations; a curse in that practically none of them are referenced and so it is difficult to know whether the person who is supposed to be the source of the quotation actually said or wrote it at all. Every effort has been made to find reliable sources for the quotations in this book; the phrase 'attributed to' is intended as a warning that we have failed to do so. The quotations concerned are all on the Internet in myriad websites and often quoted differently. Eagle-eyed and knowledgeable readers may find entertainment in letting the publisher know of any authentic sources for the 'attributed' quotations here.

Page

2   Our separateness is an illusion . . .': Laszlo, *Science and the Akashic Field*, p.7.

2   'Man who gets paid on Tuesday . . . ': attributed to Steve Allen, comedian.

5   'It's a sobering fact . . .': attributed to Tom Lehrer, songwriter.

6   'Unlike most other species . . . ': Sahtouris, *Gaia*, p.24.

7   'an intense preoccupation with power, pleasure, and love': Danesh, *Unity*, p.38.

8   'We go round . . .': Joni Mitchell, from the song 'The Circle Game'.

9   'Ignorance gives one a large range of probabilities': Eliot, *Daniel Deronda*, Book 2, Ch.13.

10   'I used to wake up at 4 a.m. and start sneezing . . .': attributed to James Thurber, writer.

12   'The unexamined life . . .': Socrates, quoted in Plato, *Dialogues*, Apology.

12   'A moment's reflection . . .': The Báb, quoted in Bahá'u'lláh, *Kitáb-i-Íqán*, p.237.

13   'the faith of no man can be conditioned . . .': Bahá'u'lláh, *Gleanings* LXXV, para.1, p.143.

14   'The injury of one shall be considered the injury of all . . .': 'Abdu'l-Bahá, *Promulgation*, p.168.

16   'The human mind is a great and wondrous thing . . .':Attributed to Kurt Vonnegut.

17   'this confession of helplessness . . .': Bahá'u'lláh, *Gleanings* LXXXIII, para.4, p.165.

17   'it is from weakness unknown . . .': Joseph Conrad, *Lord Jim*, Ch. 5.

18   'Regard man as a mine rich in gems . . .': Bahá'u'lláh, *Gleanings* CXXII, p.260.

19   'mortal man is prone to err . . .': ibid. XCIII, para.6, p.186.

21   'Some things my mom taught me . . .': Anonymous, adapted by Barry Buzza, Christian minister.

22   'Man is my mystery, and I am his mystery': the Prophet Muhammad, quoted by Bahá'u'lláh, *Gleanings* XC, para.1, p.177.

24   'For every one of you his paramount duty . . .': Bahá'u'lláh, *Gleanings* CXXIII, para.3, p.261.

24   'Man's social life is essentially a moral affair': Shotter, 'The development of personal powers'.

25   'The troubles of this world pass . . .': Letter written on behalf of Shoghi Effendi to an individual believer, 5 August 1949, in 'Living the Life', *Compilation*, vol. II, no.1322, p.20.

25   'If logic tells you . . .': attributed to Shira Milgrom.

27   'In this journey the seeker . . .': Bahá'u'lláh, *Seven Valleys*, p.5.

33   'People call me a feminist whenever . . .': Rebecca West (1892–1983), writer, article in *The Clarion*, 1913.

33   'I do not wish . . .': Mary Wollstonecraft, *A Vindication of the Rights of Women* (1792), Ch.IV, para.34.

34   'All I want is a warm bed . . .': Ashleigh Brilliant, Potshot no. 2503, www. ashleighbrilliant.com

34   'I wish men would get more in touch . . .': attributed to Betsy Salkind, comedian.

35   'It's a man's world . . .': attributed to Katherine Anne Porter (1890–1980), writer.

35   'Where a system of oppression . . .': attributed to Florynce R. Kennedy (1916–2000), civil rights lawyer.

36   'When a woman behaves like a man . . .': attributed to Dame Edith Evans, actress.

37   'Men and women, women and men . . .': attributed to Erika Jones, journalist.

40   'Why can't a woman be like a man?': Alan Lerner, *My Fair Lady*, after G.B. Shaw, *Pygmalion*.

41   'Even if man could understand woman . . .': attributed to A.W. Brown.

42   'The only way to make a husband over . . .': attributed to Mary Roberts Rinehart (1876–1957), writer.

45   'Do not look back in anger . . .': attributed to James Thurber, humourist, writer and cartoonist, quoted in Brooker, *Balanced Living*, p.242.

47   'The best things in life aren't things': attributed to Art Buchwald, humourist.

49   'No man is an island but . . .': Ashleigh Brilliant, Potshot no. 1120, www. ashleighbrilliant.com.

52   'When I was a kid . . .': attributed to Emo Philips, comedian.

52   'To pray is to pay attention to something . . .': W.H. Auden, 'Culture and Leisure', lecture delivered at the Catholic University of America, 26 February 1966.

53   'the sign of the intellect is contemplation . . .': 'Abdu'l-Bahá, *Paris Talks*, p.174.

54   'Prayer and meditation are . . .': Letter on behalf of Shoghi Effendi, in *Compilation*, vol. II, p.241.

61   'Fear is nothing but faith in reverse gear': Napoleon Hill (1883–1970), writer, quoted in Brooker, p.246.

62   'When you've exhausted all possibilities . . .': attributed to Robert H. Schuller.

65   'As you have faith . . .': 'Abdu'l-Bahá, quoted in Balyuzi, *'Abdu'l-Bahá*, p.73.

65   'The steed of this Valley is patience . . .': Bahá'u'lláh, *The Seven Valleys*, p.5.

66   'And those souls whose inner being . . .':'Abdu'l-Bahá, *Selections*, no.174, p.212.

67   'Man is under all conditions immersed . . .': ibid. no.178, p.215.

67   'Let us neither make known our sufferings nor complain . . .': ibid. no.195, p.247.

68   'Ask not of Me that which We desire not for thee . . .': Bahá'u'lláh, Hidden Words, Arabic no.18.

68   'Man's merit lieth in service and virtue . . .': Bahá'u'lláh, *Tablets*, p.138.

72   'Why the hell should I get a wife . . .': attributed to George Mitchell 'Furry' Lewis (1899–1981), musician.

73   'An archaeologist is the best husband . . .': attributed to Agatha Christie (1890–1976), mystery writer, married to archaeologist Max Mallowan.

77   'A divorce is like an amputation . . .': attributed to Margaret Atwood, novelist and poet.

78   'I am still going on bad dates . . .': attributed to Laura Kightlinger, comedian and writer.

80   'We have to realize that . . .': R.D. Laing, *The Politics of Experience*.

80   'Because the superior man seeks out difficulties . . .': Lao Tse, Tao Te Ching, no.63.

81   'We will all, verily, abide by the will of God': Bahá'u'lláh, Kitáb-i-Aqdas, p.105.

82   'All the best stories . . .': A.C. Benson, *Escape and Other Essays*, p.7.

87   'All men should try to learn before they die . . .': James Thurber, quoted in Brooker, p.253.

87   'Maturity: It's when you stop doing . . .': Marilyn Vos Savant, 'Ask Marilyn', in *Parade Magazine*.

88   'Anybody who watches three games of football . . .': attributed to Erma Bombeck (1927–96), writer and humourist.

92   'Here am I': Bahá'u'lláh, Long Obligatory Prayer, in most Bahá'í prayer books.

93   'so cleanse his heart that no remnant . . .': Bahá'u'lláh, *Kitáb-i-Íqán*, p.192; see also *Gleanings* CXXV, para.1, p.264.

98   'There is so much to be said for exotic marriages . . .':attributed to Saul Bellow (1915–2005), novelist and playwright.

99   'Like dear St Francis . . .': Oscar Wilde (1854–1900), letter written from exile, 1898.

100   'Does being born into a Christian family . . .': attributed to Corrie ten Boom (1892–1983), humanitarian.

102 'I think men who have a pierced ear . . .': attributed to Rita Rudner, comedian.

103 'Once the toothpaste is out of the tube . . .': attributed to H.R. 'Bob' Haldeman (1926–1993), White House Chief of Staff to President Nixon, imprisoned following the Watergate scandal.

104 'No person was ever honoured for what he received . . .': attributed to Calvin Coolidge (1872–1933), 30th President of the United States.

111 'Jerry had never done anything he wanted since . . .: attributed to Kate Douglas, novelist.

112 'Don't be afraid to take a big step . . .': attributed to David Lloyd George (1863–1945), statesman.

114 'Tell me about yourself . . .': Peter Arno (1904–1968), cartoonist.

115 'Don't accept rides from strange men . . .': attributed to Robin Morgan, radical feminist, writer and editor.

116 'I asked this girl out and . . .': attributed to Dom Irrera, comedian.

117 'Nothing takes the taste out of peanut butter . . .': Charlie Brown, character in the 'Peanut' cartoons by Charles M. Schulz (1922–2000).

118 'I came into my hotel room one night . . .': attributed to Groucho Marx (1890–1977), comedian, actor and writer.

123 'and you shall love the Lord your God . . .': Mark 12: 30–32.

126 'One half of the world . . .': Jane Austen (1775–1817), *Emma*.

128 'Somethin' tells me it's all happening at the zoo': Paul Simon, 'At the Zoo' (1967).

129 'People are going on dates . . .': attributed to Margot Black, writer and comedian.

130 'Natives who beat drums . . .': attributed to Mary Ellen Kelly.

134   'It is in our faults and failings . . .': Jerome K. Jerome (1859–1927), *Idle Thoughts of an Idle Fellow* (1886).

137   'Love is the free exercise of choice': M. Scott Peck, *The Road Less Traveled*, p.98.

141   'Love is a gross exaggeration . . .': attributed to George Bernard Shaw,

141   'the aim of true love is always spiritual growth': M. Scott Peck, op.cit.

142   'In a constructive marriage . . .': ibid. p. 118.

142   'sacrificial, but what is sacrificed is not the self . . .': Harville Hendrix, *Getting the Love You Want*, p. 290.

143   'People talk about "sex" as though . . .': attributed to Anne Morrow Lindbergh (1906–2001), writer.

144   'See, the probem is . . .': attributed to Robin Williams, actor.

145   'My father . . .': Katherine Hepburn (1907–2003), www.imdb.com

149   'My mother . . .': attributed to Dana Gould, comedian.

150   'Sexual intercourse began in nineteen sixty-three . . .': Philip Larkin (1922–85), 'Annus Mirabilis'.

153   'The big difference . . .': attributed to Brendan Behan (1923–64), playwright.

153   'My schoolmates . . .': attributed to Emo Philips, comedian.

154   'He that breaks a thing . . .': J.R.R.Tolkien, *The Lord of the Rings* (Gandalf to Saruman).

155   'You use sex to express every emotion except love . . .': Woody Allen, *Husbands and Wives* (Judy to Gabe).

156   'And as the human heart . . .': Bahá'u'lláh, *Gleanings* CXIV, para.15, pp.237–8.

159   'The most important thing . . .': Father Theodore M. Hesburgh (b.1917), quoted in *Readers' Digest*, January 1965.

162 'Before marriage absolutely chaste . . .': Letter on behalf of Shoghi Effendi, in *Compilation*, vol. 1, p.57.

162 'And if he met the fairest . . .': Bahá'u'lláh, *Gleanings* LX, para. 3, p.118.

164 Statistics from *Social Trends 2006*, Office for National Statistics, United Kingdom.

165 'My wife . . .': attributed to Jonathan Katz, comedian.

165 'The modern Little Red Riding Hood . . .': Marshall McLuhan, *The Mechanical Bride*.

167 'when women engage in sex . . .': Sharon Hillier, University of Pittsburgh, Magee-Women's Hospital, quoted in Angier, *Woman: An Intimate Geography*, p. 59.

168 'This wasn't conversation . . .': attributed to Edna Ferber (1995–1968), novelist.

170 'To be pure and holy in all things . . .': 'Abdu'l-Bahá, *Selections*, no.129, para. 1, p. 146.

171 'Arise, O people . . .': Bahá'u'lláh, Lawḥ-i-Dunyá (Tablet of the World), para.9, in *Tablets*, p. 86.

172 'The reason grandparents . . .': attributed to Sam Levenson (1911–1980), humourist and author.

175 'Every marriage is a battle between two families . . .': attributed to Dr Carl Whitaker (d. 1995), family therapist.

176 'I grew up to have my father's looks . . .': attributed to Jules Feiffer, cartoonist.

177 'The invention of the teenager was a mistake . . .': attributed to Judith Martin (Miss Manners), columnist and authority on etiquette.

178 'If you have never been hated by your child . . .': attributed to Bette Davis (1908–1989), actress.

182 'This great law . . .': Letter written on behalf of Shoghi Effendi, quoted in Bahá'u'lláh, *The Kitáb-i-Aqdas*, note 92, p.207.

183 'I should have known . . .': Woody Allen, 'Second Marriage', in *Woody Allen Standup Comic 1964–1968*, www.ibras.dk/comedy/allen

184 'When I was a boy of 14 . . .': attributed to Mark Twain (1835–1910), writer and humourist.

187 'Just as the earth attracts everything . . .': 'Abdu'l-Bahá, quoted in *Bahá'í Readings*, p.305.

188 'are to be regarded as the originating purpose of all creation': Bahá'u'lláh, *Gleanings* LXXIII, p.141.

190 'I was caesarean born . . .': Steven Wright, comedian, actor and writer.

191 'We spend the first twelve months . . .': attributed to Phyllis Diller, comedian.

193 'When I grow up . . .': Joseph Heller (1923–1999) satirist, author of *Catch-22*. From *Something Happened* (1974).

194 'marriage is an eternal teaching . . . which according to 'Abdu'l-Bahá will continue to be promulgated . . .': See *Bahá'í Marriage and Family Life*, p.2.

196 'Thou art even as a finely tempered sword . . .': Bahá'u'lláh, Hidden Words, Persian no.72.

197 'If you want to find out some things about yourself . . .': attributed to P.J. O'Rourke, writer.

202 'My fiancé and I are having a little disagreement . . .': attributed to Sally Poplin.

204 'It's just like magic . . .': attributed to Merrill Markoe, writer and comedian.

204 'Bad quarrels come when . . .': attributed to Betty Smith (1896–1972), novelist and dramatist.

206 'Basically my wife was immature . . .': Woody Allen, 'My Marriage', in *Woody Allen Standup Comic 1964–1968*, www.ibras.dk/comedy/allen

207 'ever improve the spiritual life of each other: 'Abdu'l-Bahá, *Selections*, no.86, p.118.

208 'The more we search for ourselves . . .': Letter written on behalf of Shoghi Effendi to an individual, 18 February 1954, in *Lights of Guidance*, p. 114.

209 'My home is the home of peace . . .': 'Abdu'l-Bahá, in *Star of the West*, Vol.XX, no.2, p.52.